Coastal Zone
Resource Management

edited by
James C. Hite
James M. Stepp

Published in cooperation with Clemson University, Clemson, South Carolina

The Praeger Special Studies program—utilizing the most modern and efficient book production techniques and a selective worldwide distribution network—makes available to the academic, government, and business communities significant, timely research in U.S. and international economic, social, and political development.

Coastal Zone Resource Management

PRAEGER SPECIAL STUDIES IN U.S. ECONOMIC AND SOCIAL DEVELOPMENT

Praeger Publishers   New York   Washington   London

PRAEGER PUBLISHERS
111 Fourth Avenue, New York, N.Y. 10003, U.S.A.
5, Cromwell Place, London S.W.7, England

Published in the United States of America in 1971
by Praeger Publishers, Inc.

All rights reserved

© 1971 by Praeger Publishers, Inc.

Library of Congress Catalog Card Number: 70-146891

Printed in the United States of America

PREFACE
by James C. Hite

THE NATURE OF THE PROBLEM

Of all the natural resource-environmental policy problems facing the American people, the most pressing appear to be centered in the Coastal Zone. Coastal resources are not as widely scattered geographically as are other natural resources. They are concentrated in a rather narrow band where the continent meets the tidal sea, and they are used by a population scattered all across the continental land mass. The pressure on these scarce coastal resources has grown with increases in population, wealth, mobility, and leisure time. With this growing pressure has come increased conflicts over who is to use the resources of the Coastal Zone, how they are to be used, and when that use is to take place. The result has been a new interest at both federal and state levels in devising a management system (or systems) for the resources of the Coastal Zone.

It is probably neither possible nor desirable to state a rigorously precise definition of the Coastal Zone. A definition that is suitable for the Maine or Oregon coast may not be suitable for the coast of Florida or Texas. In each region, the physical nature of the Coastal Zone testifies to its geological history. Along the rocky, glaciated coast north of Chesapeake Bay, the coastline is characterized by deep indentations and flooded river valleys. The areas of salt marsh are comparatively small, and the shore slopes steeply into the water.

Down the South Atlantic Coast and around the Gulf crescent, one finds relatively shallow bays, inlets, and lagoons, with miles of barrier beaches and great expanses of marshland. Along the Pacific Coasts, from California to Washington, the coastal mountains drop dramatically into the sea, creating rocky headlands between which lie short stretches of cove beaches produced by the weathering of the sea cliffs. Within each of these regions, there are areas and subareas of different geologic formations, all posing highly different management problems. A definition of the Coastal Zone that failed to account for such diversity would be misleading and counterproductive.

Yet there are some common features of Coastal Zone management problems faced by all states. Increased filling of marshlands and shallow waters, pollution from domestic and industrial wastes and agricultural chemicals, access to beach areas for recreationists, and preservation of habitat for fish and wildlife are problems that beset planners and public administrators in almost all coastal areas. The tie that binds these diverse coastal areas together is the need to resolve the conflicts over the use of uniquely coastal resources through systems of rational, scientific management.

In speaking of management systems for the resources of the Coastal Zone, one must move into the realm of political science and institutional economics. Many of the services produced by coastal resources are what economists call "public goods"; that is, they are not normally bought and sold in the market place. Moreover, the resources themselves are often "common property." There is no private ownership of an estuary, and private ownership of marshlands and beaches is extremely limited. So, although inputs from many disciplines--ecology, sociology, engineering--must be available and used in a management system for coastal resources, the basic concern here is with the creation of new, and the modification of existing, institutions within a political context. Ultimately, management decisions for the Coastal Zone will be made through political channels.

OBJECTIVES OF A MANAGEMENT SYSTEM

Rational management of the Coastal Zone requires the careful, precise identification of a set of goals or objectives. There are many legitimate objectives. The following are only a few examples:

1. To maximize the average (mean or median) pecuniary income of local people in the coastal communities

2. To maximize the hunting and fishing opportunities of coastal areas

3. To maximize the number of jobs available to people in coastal areas

4. To maximize the beauty of the coastal environment

5. To minimize changes in the natural environment.

All of these objectives (and others) may be quite proper, and they all have their proponents. But they cannot all be realized at the same time. If the choice is made to maximize the beauty of the Coastal Zone, it may not be feasible to reach the highest possible level of pecuniary income for the local area. Indeed, if all the objectives that might be enumerated were compatible with each other, there would be no management problem. Decisions must be made as to which goals or objectives are most important and at what point alternative objectives should be turned to. For example, the goal of keeping average income in the coastal area above some specified level may be choosen as most important, but, once this goal is reached, the decision may then be made to attempt to maximize hunting and fishing opportunities in the area rather than directly increasing income further. The important point is that it is not possible to have all the services of the Coastal Zone that all the people desire. Someone must define objectives and set priorities, and, again, those decisions must be made within the political process.

DEVELOPMENT OF A MANAGEMENT SYSTEM

The papers that follow discuss a wide range of issues related to developing a scientific management system for the Coastal Zone. In Part I, E. Jack Schoop, David A. Adams, and Frederick C. Marland recount the experience to date in structuring management programs. These papers describe the slow, sometimes frustrating, process of compromise and perseverance through which the American political process establishes objectives and creates institutions to administer policy. In Part II, leading authorities representing the disciplines of law, economics, planning, and ecology criticize and evaluate that political process and suggest the insights their discipline can contribute to solving the public management problem in the Coastal Zone. The comments and suggestions of these authorities are elaborated upon, and questioned by, discussants among the younger professionals in each of the disciplines.

These papers do not answer all the questions that must be answered if the Coastal Zone is to come under enlightened and vigorously effective management. But they do help to define the dimensions of a solution and move the dialogue among all the scientific disciplines involved in Coastal Zone management to a new and higher level.

INTRODUCTION

by Eugene A. Laurent
and James M. Stepp

OVERVIEW

The recent and current widespread interest in, and concern over, the quality of the environment have generated a substantial volume of literature dealing with various aspects of the problems of preserving and/or restoring various qualitative aspects of parts or sectors of the environment. The papers and discussions presented in this volume were intended to cover only those aspects of the over-all problem that are especially relevant to developing and implementing policies and programs for managing a particular kind of resource--the Coastal Zone--within a framework of economic and technological progress. Most of the problems and relationships that exist in the Coastal Zone have counterparts in other geographical areas, however; hence, the papers should be of interest to a broad spectrum of conservationists, planners, developers, and others with a personal or professional interest in the management of natural and related man-made resources.

To review, in detail, the vast range of subject matter and ideas presented in this volume would be an impossible task. Rather, the purpose here is to depict the tone of the various papers, point up some of the major ideas where a consensus seems to be indicated, and discuss further several major points where no such consensus was achieved.

Schoop, in describing the practical difficulties faced by the San Francisco Bay Conservation and Development Commission in devising and implementing a management system, delineates the problem area very well. The general tone of the papers, however, often seems somewhat broader than Coastal Zone management. Much discussion is over what could be termed "the environmental dichotomy"--conservation versus development. For example, the paper by Hufschmidt, Knox, and Parker stresses this point and ties it to resource management problems by asking how much damage to the natural system (from an industry) is acceptable in return for providing jobs and dignity for 100 poor families.

Referring to the environmental dichotomy, and specifically to Coastal Zone management, the authors' appraisals of the future range from cautious optimism to dire pessimism. Schoop offers hope by presenting a coastal management plan that has been implemented, is doing a job, and provides a guide for other plans. Adams, and Marland to a lesser extent, also offer hope in that various management plans are on the drawing boards at both state and federal levels. Marland, however, appears to feel, in general, that the social system is based on an invalid view of man's relationship with the environment and is, thus, unlikely to develop an effective coastal management plan except over a long period of time. What is needed now is the means to ensure that there will, in fact, be some coastal areas and estuaries left to manage when the country gets around to it. Hufschmidt et al. and Kissin seem to feel that an effective Coastal Zone management system is likely and probable as soon as the tools to implement such a plan are developed and environmental ignorance is dispelled.

In discussing the dynamic aspects of planning, Kissin raises an interesting point. He recognizes that any long-range plan is of dubious value and will probably have to be altered. In planning today, because of changes in knowledge, technology, and goals, the substance of tomorrow's problems are very likely being created. This situation is unavoidable, however. The test of the quality of planning today should be whether or not the problems being created for the future are less serious than those the country is attempting to solve.

Along a more specific line, Knetsch, Marland, and Ward all stress the problem of externalities and the ambiguity of property rights in marshlands and tidelands as basic sources of the dilemma regarding conservation and development. Knetsch and Marland recommend a system of resource taxes in an effort to force developers to account for all of the costs of their actions. A large majority of the authors, however, lean toward institutional and political action rather than markets as a means of correcting the property-rights problem.

CURRENT AND PROPOSED MANAGEMENT SYSTEMS

The three papers presented by Schoop, Adams, and Marland prepare the foundation for the remainder of the papers. Although these papers deal with management at different levels of government, all three agree upon several basic points:

1. Present governmental arrangements in the Coastal Zone are inadequate, and sometimes detrimental, and, therefore, some kind of Coastal Zone authority needs to be established to overcome the present fragmented governmental jurisdictions in the area.

2. For the above to be politically feasible, strong and continuing public support must be generated, although this may be difficult to obtain.

3. Legislation passed to date, both at the federal and state level, is too weak to provide for a fully comprehensive coastal management program.

4. Whatever Coastal Zone management

legislation is signed into law at the various levels of government must necessarily take into account the unique characteristics of the Coastal Zone environment and the interest in this environment of the other levels of government, as well as private citizens.

In addition to these points, some relevant information is presented by Adams. Referring to several bills that have been introduced in the Senate and House of Representatives, he predicts that any Coastal Zone management legislation passed at the federal level will be based on the following principles:

1. The federal government will not fund a program that appears doomed to failure because the program lacks the capability to perform the task.

2. The states will have maximum latitude to develop programs to meet the special requirements of their areas.

3. The public will be aware of the planning process and will have ample opportunity to review and contribute to the plan as it develops.

SYNTHESIS AND COMMENT

In commenting on the management systems described in the first three papers, the authors of the other papers agree that there has been a growing and necessary concern for the preservation of coastal resources and that this is a welcome change from the belief that these resources are of no value unless they can be developed. They are not, however, in agreement as to exactly who should assume the responsibility for the management of these resources.

There is general agreement that local government

should be given consideration in any management plan, but there also seems to be a consensus that a truly comprehensive coastal management system cannot take place at this level of government. There is no clear consensus regarding the respective roles of state and federal levels of government. The importance of this ambiguity lies in the scope of the management problem and the type of data needed to implement a management system.

As one moves to higher levels of government, the scope of a management system necessarily must broaden. On a state level, much as on the local level, the important relationships are between a particular activity and its effects on the environment. Consideration must also be given to competing economic activities, as well as the relative "efficiency" of particular sites, as compared with competing sites for proposed investments. Yet, generally, despite the major exceptions in certain metropolitan coastal areas, both competing activities and alternative sites will be few in number. In addition, the variation among types of coastal environments will be slight, and environmental effects can be specified in considerable detail.

On a federal level, however, variables related to the composition of the total population, as well as specific segments of this population, become relevant variables in decision-making. Decisions must be made regarding interstate and interregional conflicts of interest. Obviously, such decisions can be made only with a loss of detail at the local level.* Thus, for example, in comparing the effect of an economic activity on a local environment, much more detail about environmental effects is possible when the alternative number of sites is three than when it is thirty-three. Some consensus needs to be

---

*Walter Isard et al., Ecologic-Economic Analysis for Regional Development (Cambridge, Mass.: Harvard University, Department of Landscape Architecture, December, 1968), pp. 413-22.

developed concerning the coastal resources management roles of various levels of government. Regardless of which level of government is given primary responsibility, conflicts of interest will remain; hence, an orderly process of making decisions about these conflicts should be developed and agreed upon before specific conflicts arise.

Although a restructuring of the market is suggested as an alternative to a permit or zoning system as a means of managing coastal resources, the role of property rights in such systems is left unresolved. Basically, private-property rights are merely a means society uses to achieve an internalization of the externalities involved in common-property rights, and new definitions of property rights arise in response to changing conditions and circumstances.* Society's new "awareness" may well necessitate a restructuring of property rights in the Coastal Zone. Extreme care, however, must be taken to ensure "equity"--that is, to ensure that some property owners do not lose property without compensation. Otherwise, the effectiveness and viability of the management plan may be endangered by legal or political attacks upon it.

In general, the authors of the various papers seem to feel that any approach to Coastal Zone management must incorporate the concept of "multiple use"; that is, the resources of the Coastal Zone are subject to utilization by a large number of activities, and some accommodation or balancing between uses must take place. The problem in determining the "proper" activities for different areas of the Coastal Zone lies in the difficulty of developing cost and benefit data for each of the alternative activities. This difficulty is compounded by three factors:

---

*Harold Demsetz, "Toward a Theory of Property Rights," American Economic Review (May, 1967), p. 350.

1. The problem of quantifying amenity or environmental values

2. The lack of available information necessary to estimate costs and benefits under alternative economic and biological conditions

3. The fact that some activities are practically irreversible and have a drastic effect on the natural environment. For example, the filling of marshes for residential purposes has a much more serious long-run ecological effect than does the discharge of domestic sewage into the same marsh area.

Unfortunately, none of the papers specifically discusses the means of overcoming these difficulties in attempting to implement a coastal management system. Several approaches to the resolution of these difficulties can be mentioned, however.

At the minimum, a traditional benefit-cost study of the major users of Coastal Zone resources in an area might be conducted, utilizing whatever information is available and expressing environmental costs in nonmonetary terms (such as acres of marsh filled or pounds of Biological Oxygen Demand [BOD] discharged). Another method would be to employ a systems approach similar to that discussed by Hufschmidt et al.; however, this approach requires large quantities of data, and, with only a little additional effort, data can be generated for what may be a better approach.

If the management of natural coastal resources is viewed as a materials-balance problem, a general economic-ecological model utilizing input-output analysis can be developed. Materials, in such a model, are seen as moving from the natural environment into the processing and consuming sectors of the economy and, from there, back into the natural environment via a series of economic-ecological linkages. These economic-ecological linkages can be quantified by modifying the input-output model to allow for interregional trading. In this model, however, the "regions" are not geographic entities, but, rather, the economic system and the natural-environment, or ecological, system. In other words, the flow of materials from the natural-environment system into the economic system and back to the environment is conceived of as a special type of import-export activity that can be thought of as intersystem trading between the economy and the ecosystem.

Such a model can be used to estimate the "environmental costs" of the economic benefits provided by various industrial, commercial, and governmental activities, including secondary or indirect environmental costs (for example, the amounts of various kinds of water or air pollutants generated per dollar of income or per full-time job).* These estimates can, in turn, be used to estimate the economic-opportunity costs, or benefits foregone, involved in reserving or making available various Coastal Zone resources and areas for nonpecuniary "environmental" uses. Such an estimate would provide the public sector with something similar to a "supply price" as that term is used in referring to the private sector of the economy; that is, it would designate the minimum value that a nonpecuniary environmental benefit must have to justify the resource being used to produce that benefit.

In addition, willingness-to-pay studies can be conducted to estimate (perhaps with a wide margin of error) the "demand price"; that is, the maximum sacrifices that users of coastal resources are willing to make in order to obtain or continue the use

---

*E.A. Laurent, "An Input-Output Study: Economic-Ecologic Linkages in the Charleston Metropolitan Region" (unpublished Ph.D. dissertation, Agricultural Economics Department, Clemson University, Clemson, S.C., December, 1970).

of coastal resources to provide nonpecuniary environmental services. These two "prices" would provide an estimate of the amount of net gain or loss that a community or a region must forego in order to maintain its coastal resources in various levels of preservation as contrasted with various kinds of development.

This extremely limited and brief discussion of economic models is only an attempt to indicate that there are, in fact, tools and methodologies available for implementing Coastal Zone management strategies if society is willing to bear the cost of generating the needed data. It should be remembered, however, that such models are only crude devices and should not be expected to serve as mechanistic substitutes for human judgment. The final decisions about the coastal environment will be made by men. Hopefully, these men will use all the scientific inputs available and will approach the problem of coastal resource management in a systematic, comprehensive fashion. Yet no model, regardless of its complexity, can fully account for all of man's emotional and psychic needs. Neither can experience, wisdom, and intuitive common sense alone serve these needs. Rather, they are all needed to deal with problems of resource allocation in the Coastal Zone.

Essentially, the papers presented in this book suggest a broadening of the concept of planning, whether it be on a regional, state, or national basis. Planning for the Coastal Zone can no longer be primarily concerned with the management and the development of the local economy under consideration; it must also take cognizance of the effect of this economic development on the coastal environment. Also, whatever type of management system is proposed must be, to a very substantial extent, people oriented. Man and his society are functioning elements of the coastal environment. Indeed, the entire purpose of managing coastal resources is to ensure that some of these resources are left for man's future enjoyment. Consequently, a management system cannot make decisions as to the location of economic activities solely on the basis of an activity's biological and ecological effects. An effective coastal management plan, in specifying what natural resources are to be preserved, must not value these resources on their ecological values alone; it must also consider their economic value as inputs to developing areas and their ability to generate pecuniary income through this development.

CONTENTS

Page

PREFACE
by James C. Hite   v

INTRODUCTION
by Eugene A. Laurent and James M. Stepp   ix

          PART I: CURRENT AND PROPOSED
                    MANAGEMENT SYSTEMS

Chapter

1   THE SAN FRANCISCO BAY EXPERIENCE
    by E. Jack Schoop   3

        Goals and Objectives   4
        Tools for Implementing the Plan   8
        Additional Political Considerations   12
        Summary   18

2   MANAGEMENT SYSTEMS UNDER CONSIDERATION AT
    THE FEDERAL-STATE LEVEL
    by David A. Adams   20

        History of the Coastal Zone Management
            Idea   20
        Bills Before the 91st Congress   22
        Features of the Administration Proposal   23
        The Coordination Problem   28
        The Role of Federal Agencies   29
        Prospects for Enactment   30
        Note   32

3   MANAGEMENT SYSTEMS UNDER CONSIDERATION AT
    THE STATE-LOCAL LEVEL: THE SOUTH ATLANTIC
    COAST
    by Frederick C. Marland   33

Chapter	Page

Federal Efforts and Scope of the Problem 33
Legalisms and a New Philosophy of Law 35
The Georgia Experience 37
The South Carolina Controversy 38
Army Corps of Engineers Permit System 39
Summary 42
Notes 43

PART II: POLICY CONSIDERATIONS

4 LEGAL AND INSTITUTIONAL CONSIDERATIONS
by Milton S. Heath, Jr. 49

The Federal Setting 49
The State Setting 50
The Local and Regional Setting 52
Some Models of Alternative Institutional Arrangements 53
   A Local Management Model 54
   A State Management Model 57
   A Federal Management Model 60
   A Multiple-Jurisdiction Management Model 62
   A Litigation Model 68
Conclusion 69

ANALYSIS, by H. Gary Knight 70

The Effect of OCS Activities on Adjacent Coastal Areas 70
The Coastal Zone As Comtemplated in Current Legislation 73
Current Law and Procedure Ameliorating Nonconsideration of OCS Management Policies 75
A Proposal 79
Conclusion 81
Notes 81

5 ECONOMICS AND MANAGEMENT OF COASTAL ZONE RESOURCES
by Jack L. Knetsch 84

Economic Nature of the Problem 85

Chapter		Page
	Nonmarket Solutions	87
	An Alternative Approach: Market Simulation	88
	Research Needs	90
	Institutional Arrangements	91
	Public Subsidies and Environmental Degradation	92
	Summary	93
	Notes	93
	ANALYSIS, by William A. Ward	95
	The Questions of Property Rights	95
	Who Bears the Cost?	97
	Geographic Distribution of Income	99
	Changing Concepts of Private Property	100
	Notes	103
6	A POLICY ANALYSIS APPROACH: OBJECTIVES, ALTERNATIVE DEVELOPMENT STRATEGIES, AND ECONOMETRIC MODELS by Maynard M. Hufschmidt, Hugh W. Knox, and Francis H. Parker	104
	The Role of Policy Analysis	105
	Objectives and Alternative Developmental Strategies	109
	Econometric Models	113
	Summary	117
	Notes	119
	ANALYSIS, by John Kissin	121
	The Need for Flexibility	121
	Limitations of Long-Range Planning	123
	Data Needs	124
	Note	126
7	ECOLOGICAL CONSIDERATIONS by Arthur W. Cooper	127
	Basic Ecological Considerations in the Coastal Zone	128

Chapter	Page
Man's Interactions with Coastal Zone Ecosystems	131
A Coastal Zone Management System with an Ecological Basis	133
Notes	140
ANALYSIS, by Norbert Dee	141
Discussion	142
A Proposed Method of Environmental Evaluation	144
Notes	146

APPENDIXES

Appendix A:	Corps of Engineers, U.S. Army News Release on Revised Navigable Waters Permit Regulations	151
Appendix B:	Descriptions of Illustrative State Programs of Estuarine Conservation by Milton S. Heath, Jr.	154

ABOUT THE CONTRIBUTORS — 167

PART I

CURRENT AND PROPOSED MANAGEMENT SYSTEMS

CHAPTER 1

THE SAN FRANCISCO BAY EXPERIENCE

by E. Jack Schoop

Without outside intervention, as in so many other estuaries around the United States, the marshes and mudflats around San Francisco Bay were being obliterated and the San Francisco Bay system was being narrowed to become, ultimately, just a wide river. The process was stopped in San Francisco Bay, however, and the Bay is being managed today. Indeed, the San Francisco Bay Conservation and Development Commission is often cited as a model that can be emulated elsewhere. But the management system is still so young, and still so politically sensitive, that this discussion will deal with it largely in the political context in which it rests.

The biggest single realization of those involved in coastal resource management has been that nothing can presently be accomplished without strong public support (which can be translated into political support). Indeed, the whole current political thrust concerning the environment has occurred only because enough people became involved in the issue. What it takes to manage a resource like the Coastal Zone requires a considerable change in values and a considerable challenge to entrenched private interests. It requires a change from the American frontier value that constant economic and population growth in every city is both good and necessary. Much of the country's swampland, much of its coastal environment, was long ago sold to private interests that only now are in a position to reap the economic rewards, since urban growth pressures have increased their property values.

Today's effort must be directed at temporarily stopping the specific destructive actions, while the long-term effort is made to change the values and redress the legal, economic, and property system that is still dedicated primarily to taming, overcoming--indeed, obliterating--the natural environment. This means a continuing public involvement in, and understanding of, the problems of the environment-- and, in this case, the estuarine environment in particular. It means a gradual change in the views-- indeed, the values--of those substantial interests whose natural inclination is to put private rights above public rights and to put immediate growth ahead of the long-term implications of growth. It is in that context that the goals and objectives of the San Francisco Bay Commission must be understood.

GOALS AND OBJECTIVES

The basic objectives of the Commission are stated in its Bay Plan. They are (a) to protect the Bay as a great natural resource for the benefit of present and future generations <u>and</u> (b) to develop the Bay and its shoreline to their highest potential with a minimum of Bay filling. These two objectives summarize a whole gamut of more-detailed findings and policies, for what the Commission found in assembling its plan was that <u>all desirable high-priority uses</u> of the Bay and its shoreline can be fully accommodated <u>without</u> major additional fill and without eliminating large natural-resource areas. That is, the plan provides fully for water-related industry, ports, water-related parks, marinas, beaches, fishing piers, salt ponds and other diked wetlands that surround San Francisco Bay, and some airports.

THE SAN FRANCISCO BAY EXPERIENCE

The plan allows for some fill for these high-priority uses and also minor amounts to improve shoreline attractiveness and to provide public access. But it prescribes that filling should be limited to these purposes--and should be the very minimum needed for the specific purposes--because the Bay is needed in essentially its present form to protect fish and wildlife, to help fight water pollution, and to help maintain the present fine climate of the Bay Area. This means no more fill for housing, or just to get rid of refuse, or because this area is the easiest place to put a freeway these days.

All this is set forth in a list of carefully worded policies about each of these vital subjects. And the act of the Legislature that made the Commission a permanent agency in 1969 also legally established those policies as the Commission's "Bible," with which any future filling or dredging in the Bay must be in accord. For example, with regard to water pollution, the Commission found that key elements that affect flushing and the supply of dissolved oxygen (to permit the elimination of degradable wastes) are (a) the volume of water flowing in and out with the tides (and fresh water flowing into the Bay), (b) the temperature of Bay waters, and (c) the rates of oxygen interchange at the surface of the Bay, including tidal flats. Thus, its policy is that, to the greatest extent feasible, the remaining marshes and mudflats around the Bay, the remaining water volume and surface area of the Bay, and the fresh water inflow into the Bay should be maintained. These are not the Commission's only policies on water pollution, however, but merely one of five summary findings and one of three summary policies.

With regard to marshes and mudflats, it found that most marine life in the Bay either depends directly on the marshes and mudflats for its sustenance or depends indirectly upon them by feeding upon other marine life so nourished. Shore birds also depend upon the marshes and mudflats for both food and shelter. Thus, its policy is that marshes and mudflats should be maintained to the fullest extent possible to conserve fish and wildlife and to abate air and water pollution. Filling and diking that eliminate marshes and mudflats should, therefore, be allowed only for purposes providing substantial public benefits and only if there is no reasonable alternative. Marshes and mudflats are an integral part of the Bay tidal system and, therefore, should be protected in the same manner as open water areas.

The above are representative samples of some of the policies concerning <u>conservation</u> of the Bay. A few policies concerning the needs of economic <u>development</u> around the rim of the Bay follow. With regard to water-oriented industry (that is, industry that requires frontage on navigable waters to receive raw materials and/or to distribute processed materials by ship), the Commission found that such industry is basic to the economy of the Bay Area and the western United States; therefore, the needs of water-related industry must be given high priority in the Bay Plan. Thus, its policy is that, because shoreline land suitable for water-related industry will eventually become scarce, such land should be reserved now specifically for this purpose. The amount of additional land to be reserved should be determined on the basis of the best data available, using a fifty-year planning period to anticipate future needs as well as possible. In addition, water-related industrial sites should be planned so as to avoid wasteful use of the limited supply of waterfront land. Some detailed site-design specifications are then listed in the policy, followed by the policy conclusion that some filling may be necessary at some sites, despite the most careful attention to proper site layout.

With regard to airports, one of the Commission's findings was that the shoreline of the Bay is a favored location for airports because the Bay provides an open space for takeoffs and landings away from populated areas. A Bay shore location is also conveniently close to present population centers. The high potential Bay fill requirements of airports were noted, and the following basic policy was adopted: "To enable the Bay Area to have adequate airport facilities and to minimize the harmful effects of

THE SAN FRANCISCO BAY EXPERIENCE

airport expansion upon the Bay, a regional airport system plan should be prepared at the earliest time by a responsible regional agency."

Because airport planning had been on a highly competitive single-airport basis in the past and since efforts to get a comprehensive regional study had been constantly stymied, the Commission put the following teeth in its policy:

> It is assumed that three years will be needed to complete an adequate regional airport system plan, and as many as five to seven years thereafter to build facilities proposed in the plan. Therefore, pending completion of the comprehensive airport system plan, capital investment in, and any Bay filling for, major airports in the Bay region should be limited to improvements needed within the next 10 years (i.e., before 1979).

After a long delay, work on a regional airport-system plan for the Bay Area has been started.

After treating its "priority" uses of the Bay--water-related industry, ports, water-related parks, marinas, beaches, fishing piers, salt ponds and other diked wetlands, and airports--the Commission noted that the shoreline of the Bay is used for a wide variety of other uses and concluded with the following policies:

> Shore areas not proposed to be reserved for a priority use should be used for any purpose (acceptable to the local government having jurisdiction) that uses the Bay as an asset and in no way affects the Bay adversely. . . . Types of development that could not use the Bay as an asset (and therefore should not be allowed in shoreline areas) include: (a) refuse disposal (except as it may be found to be suitable for an approved fill), (b) use of deteriorated structures for low-rent

storage or other non-water-related purposes, and (c) junkyards.

TOOLS FOR IMPLEMENTING THE PLAN

Fortunately, the state legislation that created the original, temporary Bay Commission in 1965 directed it to (a) prepare a plan that would be "enforceable" and (b) prescribe the tools needed to do the enforcing. Having seen the need for effective action as it surveyed the existing problem, the Commission did not hesitate to recommend that a permanent regional agency be established to carry out the Bay Plan. It recommended that the agency be given continued control over filling and dredging and also additional controls over developments on the shoreline that, unregulated, would either despoil the Bay shore or, by wasteful misuse of prime waterfront land, cause future pressure for avoidable fills in the Bay. It also recommended a continuing review of the Bay Plan as a key to perpetuating its final unspecified, but very effective, tool--education and persuasion.

For a truly effective regional agency, the Commission recommended a limited regional government. Only a comprehensive regional government could plan and operate regional transportation systems, acquire regional open space, and reserve prime industrial lands on the scale deemed necessary to prevent continued pressure to fill the Bay for these purposes. Failing that, the Commission recommended a permanent special-purpose Bay agency that would be designed to meld into a regional government when at last it was created.

Under the adopted Bay Plan policies, the single-purpose agency could still try to be the tail that wagged the dog and try to force more-rational airport or surface transportation planning by denying fill for these purposes, but that would be a dog-wagging exercise; the airport or the freeway interests might pick up more political muscle and somehow override the Bay agency, or the congestion that might result could generate an overpowering storm of

THE SAN FRANCISCO BAY EXPERIENCE   9

public protest, or future members of the Commission
could even decide to yield merely in anticipation of
such consequences.

   In 1969, the Commission was made a permanent
agency until arrangements for a proper regional
government could be successfully completed and the
necessary legislation could be passed. In the new
legislation, the Commission was authorized to continue
its control over filling and dredging--with the Bay
Plan policies officially established as the Commission's guide. In a sharp political fight, the seem-
ing impossibility of asserting some regional control
over shoreline land use in conjunction with local
zoning power was partially overcome.

   The Commission had recommended that the permanent
agency have shared juridiction with local governments
over the entire area of its priority areas as actually
mapped in the Bay Plan--that is, over all the port,
airport, industrial, and park lands that it had
mapped--plus shared jurisdiction over the first tier
of properties adjoining the remainder of the Bay
shore. Bay agency jurisdiction over the priority
areas was, of course, to assure their proper use and
thus avoid waste of the resource. Jurisdiction in
the case of the rest of the shoreline was (a) to
assure that maximum public access to the Bay could
be required in every feasible case and (b) to assure
that the use, whatever it was, treated the Bay as an
asset--that is, addressed the Bay, used it as a
design asset, and did not simply back up to the Bay,
ignoring it as a sort of derelict area, as was so
often done in the past.

   What survived the political give and take was
control over the first 100 feet back from the Bay,
regardless of whether it was a priority or nonpriority
area. Within the 100-foot band, the permanent commission can attempt to order the proper use of
priority areas--a dubious possibility at best, given
only 100 feet--and it can require maximum feasible
public access as part of development or redevelopment.
It was not authorized to pursue its second objective--
seeing that proper use is made of the shore, whatever

the use--but that was not considered a tragic loss for reasons that will be explained below. The big accomplishments, of course, were the authority to require public access to the Bay in private developments and the establishment of the principle of shared regional and local jurisdiction, however small 100 feet might be. It is hoped that it will not be too long before the need for a more workable area of shared jurisdiction will be apparent enough to foster its enactment.

The final "tool," the nonlegislatable one to which the Commission basically owes its present life and through which it will successfully carry on, if properly used, is education and persuasion. For it was the Commission's very logical, but too seldom used, method of planning and decision-making that made the Commission, its problem, and its recommendations the best-known and the most successfully fought-for issue in the 1969 California Legislature.

What the Commission did was to take a large and complex problem, both physical and governmental, and break it down into twenty-five tangible and plausible categories.* Each issue was separately and equally considered, one after another. Each issue received its own separate hearing; it was never lost among, or demeaned by, the whole array of issues involved. Not only was each subject considered separately; it was also considered in depth and by the largest possible number of participants, especially affected parties who might be expected to oppose the Commission's recommendations on the subject.

---

*The categories are as follows: tidal movement; sedimentation; pollution; fish and wildlife; marshes and mudflats; flood control; smog and weather; salt, sand, shells, and water; appearance and design; geology; fill; economic and population growth; ports; airports; transportation; recreation; waterfront industry; waterfront housing; public facilities and utilities; refuse disposal; ownership; powers; government; review of barrier proposals; and oil and gas production.

THE SAN FRANCISCO BAY EXPERIENCE

On each subject, a technical report was prepared--either by a specialized consultant or an in-house person. A simple summary of about ten to twelve pages, in the plainest possible language, was then prepared by the staff for simultaneous publication. Finally, even the summaries were boiled down to a single sheet of mimeographed "possible conclusions." These conclusions represented the substance of the subject, which was deemed important enough, at that point, to be included in the final Bay Plan when it was compiled.

Long before it went to the full Commission and to the public, each report was reviewed by affected parties and by an interdisciplinary advisory committee, and was revised as necessary. Only then was it published, accompanied by a two-page press release summarizing the substance and clearly indicating the basic conclusions on which the Commission was going to be asked to vote. This process--plus the fact that this was an agency with police power that was going to make some decisions as to how it was going to exercise its police function--resulted in widespread press coverage and maximum possible exposure, month after month, as one report followed another. The final act in each case was Commission review, modification, and adoption of the "possible conclusions" from the report. In this manner, the Commission and the public had maximum participation in making the decisions on <u>each</u> issue.

At the end of the process, the adopted conclusions were amalgamated into a composite Plan Report-- with surprisingly little conflict and adjustment, because the Commission began to resolve some of the potential conflicts as it went along. (For instance, in considering freeways, it decided then and there that they had to be kept out of the Bay if at all possible, and the policies under which they might possibly be allowed were hammered out then--not in the assembled plan.) The final plan was then published in preliminary form, widely reviewed, and discussed, whereupon the Commission hammered out the final wording of every paragraph and approved it by a nearly unanimous vote.

This exhaustive process worked so well that a gradual change of attitude occurred in many local governments and in the citizenry all around the Bay. Gradually, an impressive number of local governments and property owners began to seek and promote only good-quality shoreline developments. And gradually they realized that, in a sensitive environmental system, the misdeeds of a brother city miles away up the Bay could adversely affect them, and the need for an effective regional agency was widely endorsed by local governments. Two cities and two counties even went so far as to endorse shoreline controls in the face of their previous parochialism.

That is why the Commission is not too concerned that any city today is going to allow wanton abuse of its shoreline by any owner, even though it has no power over that problem itself, and that is why it places a great deal of emphasis upon a continuing review of the Bay Plan--so it can continue the process of again focusing on each issue in turn and can refresh everyone's thinking about it, especially that of the affected decision-makers.

ADDITIONAL POLITICAL CONSIDERATIONS

Usually, the most crucial political consideration is the concern that "home-rule" local governments have about any curtailment of their powers. The Commission largely overcame this problem by working very closely with local government officials and the general concerned public, thereby convincing them of the regional nature of the problem and winning their support for a regional agency to handle it. The principal point that this demonstrates is the crucial necessity of gradually developing the solution to a problem in a clear and open fashion and as fully in partnership with the affected parties as it is physically possible to do.

Another very important political consideration is that 25 per cent of what remains of San Francisco Bay is claimed by private owners, and another 25 per cent has been given to cities to develop ports and a variety of other economic developments. The size and composition of the Commission is also a problem, as is the problem of money to run the agency and to carry out the Bay Plan.

The problems of San Francisco Bay began about 100 years ago when the spirit of the land was to tame the West and to foster the growth of strong new cities. Both the state and the federal governments were diligent in selling off so-called swamp and overflow lands to be filled and developed. It was not until the turn of the century that the disposition program was slowed. Since then many of the claims in San Francisco Bay have been assembled by a few, very large landholders, all politically powerful.

One alternative is to buy the private holdings in the Bay, but, in a large though indeterminable number of cases, this seems to be unnecessary. The Commission found that many of the claims apparently could be proved to have been fraudulently obtained and also that many were subject to a form of easement called the "public trust for fisheries, commerce, and navigation," which easement or "trust" would preclude them from being filled. In addition, the Commission was advised by legal counsel that its studies had proven that there is a strong public necessity to keep the Bay system as large as possible and that this public necessity was superior to the rights of private owners, so that the Commission, by regulation alone, could legally preclude private Bay lands from being filled.

The Commission decided not to base its plan on this legal argument, however, but instead resolved the dilemma by adopting policies requiring a good title check before any dubious lands would be entitled to any consideration for filling. It realized, too, that some of the lands might be able to be used economically for some of the necessary uses acknowledged in the Bay Plan, such as ports and marinas. But, under strong pressure from the owners, it also added a provision whereby such private lands could be developed for a combination of public recreation (beaches, parks, and the like) and Bay-oriented commercial recreation and Bay-oriented public assembly (defined as facilities specifically designed to attract large numbers of people to enjoy the Bay and its shoreline, such as restaurants, specialty shops, and hotels).

To this escape clause, the Commission added a number of conditions that would hopefully tend to circumscribe it and keep it from being badly abused. One of these was that a substantial portion of the project must be built on existing land. The implicit purpose was to attempt to allow owners just enough potential for some kind of economic use to avoid questions of inverse condemnation, under which the owners could claim their lands were in effect "taken" from them by the public.

The question of effect on private Bay landowners was bitterly debated in the State Legislature in 1969, when it decided the future of the Bay, but the final legislation left the Commission's policies virtually intact. The opposition did get a number of amendments into the bill, but thus far they do not appear to undermine the effectiveness of the Commission seriously.

Fortunately, there is no immediate pressure to fill and develop all the privately claimed lands at once. Probably, in the years to come, the public interest will gradually be accepted as being much greater than the private interest, and gradually the owners will write off or write down their claims. The crucial question today is whether a critical test of the policy can be postponed until then. So far, fortunately, Commission policies, combined with current economic demand for uses that the Commission would permit, are sufficient to allow current prospective developers to do something and thus postpone the question.

Concerning the areas of the Bay in effect owned by the cities for development purposes, one can appreciate how much cities valued that potential development resource. It was not something they had

THE SAN FRANCISCO BAY EXPERIENCE

paid for, however, and it was only "loaned" to them "in trust" by the state. In most cases, the interest that was aroused concerning the Bay convinced city fathers, at the behest of their constituents, to forgo improper development of those holdings. And, in time, many of the undeveloped grants can gradually be terminated or otherwise controlled; time will be required because each one has to be considered separately, particularly with regard to whether some uses of the property can be made within the spirit of the Bay Plan policies.

This does not mean that every local government goes along happily with the Commission. For example, two small, very parochial cities made a vigorous effort in the Legislature and successfully got exemptions from controls for two projects that they envisioned. In addition, ports in San Francisco Bay--like ports almost everywhere in the United States--are subsidized by leasing port lands for private real estate developments, some port-related and some not. The Commission is, therefore, under tremendous pressure to allow fills for nonport-related purposes just to subsidize the ports.

With regard to the size of the Commission, both the original Commission created in 1965 and the present Commission have 27 members. The legislation specifies who appoints each member. Seven are "public" members--five appointed by the Governor, including the chairman and the vice-chairman of the Commission, and two appointed by leaders in the State Assembly and the State Senate. Two are federal officers, representing the Army Corps of Engineers and the Department of Health, Education, and Welfare. Five are representatives of various state agencies that have an interest in the Bay, such as the Regional Water Quality Control Board; and thirteen (almost one half) are appointed from local governments around the Bay--one from each of the nine counties abutting the Bay and four mayors or councilmen appointed by the Association of Bay Area Governments.

Four years of experience with the original Commission showed that, although this array of officials was representative of a whole range of interests, no groups of Commissioners congealed into special interest groups. With no pressure to form blocks, each Commissioner voted his own mind, which meant that most of the time he voted for the regional interest and for the environment, instead of for the more parochial interest group from which he might have been appointed.

Are twenty-seven members hard to manage? They could be, but, in this case, they were not. Part of the credit for this goes to a good chairman, who kept everyone's eye on the ball, and part may well go to the particular planning process that was used, which, together with the permit power, kept the Commissioners very involved as individuals and thus kept their interest up and their focus intact. The structure worked so well--especially in keeping the public interest ahead of the special interest--that the temporary Commission took special pains to recommend that, if a regional government were not created to take over the job, the continuing special agency should be constituted with appointed members in essentially the same array. That view prevailed, and the new legislation essentially just amended the old law and made the Commission permanent in its then-existing form.

Finally, regarding fiscal problems, the Commission has operated on less than $250,000 per year, and that is all that can be expected for the foreseeable future. Obviously, all one can do with that amount of money is regulate, persuade, and plan just enough to keep the Bay Plan from becoming out-of-date and unusable too quickly. There is not quite enough money to do everything that is needed in regulating development and there is _no_ money for acquiring any properties for wildlife preserves, parks, or the private Bay lands referred to above. Like most government agencies today, the Commission is feeling the budget pinch and the taxpayer revolt. It even counts itself lucky that it got a small budget increase this year while most other programs were being cut back or were held at previous levels in order to hold the line on state spending.

THE SAN FRANCISCO BAY EXPERIENCE

Fortunately, the Bay Commission is so unique, responsive, and effective--even in the Bay Area--that people will <u>donate</u> a great deal of their time and effort in order to help "save the Bay." Consultants work for the Commission for $1,000 and $3,000 contracts, actually spending much more time on their work than that amount usually covers. Some of the most eminent engineers and geologists in the country are giving their time free to serve as a Fill Safety Review Board, a pioneering effort to verify engineering analyses concerning earthquake and other potential hazards. Several equally prominent designers and landscape architects are similarly devoting their time in critical evaluation of development projects with an eye to helping the Commission make development around San Francisco Bay as attractive as its settting deserves.

Donations are also helping to make up for the lack of money to buy critically needed lands for future public use or just to prevent filling that should not take place. The Nature Conservancy has an active program around the Bay. A full-time staff is obtaining donations of land and money with which to buy other lands. The Conservancy is concentrating on key Bay lands and marshes where there are imminent pressures for fills.

But donations cannot do it all, obviously. Where the pressure for development is most acute, prices are too high for the Nature Conservancy to touch. In addition, there are a number of shoreside parks in the Bay Plan, all of which are also on local plans, but half of which are not yet on anyone's foreseeable capital budget. It is generally recognized that a regional agency is going to have to come in to assist, but neither the Commission nor any other over-all regional agency has the funds or the authority to do so.

Again, time is the Commission's biggest ally. In many cases, there are no immediate development pressures to worry about at the moment. In others, the new attitude, plus public hearings before a continuously watchful public, is resulting in new

Bayfront developments--public and private--that provide many more public benefits than previously. That is probably how the Commission will have to continue to operate for a few years. No one sees a break in the tough tax picture before that. But ultimately, sooner or later, there will probably be a limited regional government that will have a little more adequate resources.

SUMMARY

The San Francisco Bay Conservation and Development Commission may be of value as a model elsewhere, especially the following features:

1. Its large, varied composition, which represents many interests but is dominated by no special interests

2. Its police power, which includes control over filling and dredging and some aspects of shoreline development

3. Its geographic area of jurisdiction, which is large enough to cover most issues of a regional scale but small enough so that the public can fully understand and support it

4. Its concern for nurturing and keeping extensive public support and understanding as a necessary foundation for political support--by breaking issues into understandable portions, dealing with them openly and always in the clearest possible language, and always aiming at keeping the public informed and concerned. These factors are the most important of all.

No political battles are easy. None are won quickly, and some are not won permanently. The San Francisco Bay system shrank from over 700 square miles to a little more than 400 square miles in a little over 100 years. Today, at least, it is enjoying a "stay of execution." Until the test of time proves otherwise, the Commission is a workable model of a management system.

CHAPTER 2

MANAGEMENT SYSTEMS UNDER CONSIDERATION AT THE FEDERAL-STATE LEVEL

by David A. Adams

HISTORY OF THE COASTAL ZONE MANAGEMENT IDEA

The concept of a federal-state system for managing the natural resources of the nation's Coastal Zone probably began with consideration of Michigan Congressman John D. Dingell's H.R. 13447 (89th Congress) in 1966. This bill stimulated little interest at the state level, was the subject of three days of hearings, was reported favorably by the House Committee on Merchant Marine and Fisheries, and failed to pass the full House under suspension of the rules by only three votes. Although the bill failed to pass the Congress, it did have a beneficial effect; it caused people to begin thinking about a national coastal management system, and it alerted them to Congressman Dingell's intent to introduce a similar bill early in the 90th Congress.

The reception of this second effort--H.R. 25 (90th Congress)--was an entirely different matter. During the intervening year, several things had happened:

1. Opposition to dredging in the Hempstead, Long Island, area and to the

FEDERAL-STATE MANAGEMENT SYSTEMS

Corps of Engineers permit system had intensified.

2. The Sport Fishing Institute, League of Women Voters, Isaac Walton League, Conservation Foundation, and other conservation groups had initiated or expanded information campaigns.

3. The San Francisco Bay Conservation and Development Commission had begun working toward a comprehensive, enforceable plan for the conservation of the waters of San Francisco Bay and the development of its shoreline.

4. Landmark wetland-protection legislation and subsequent court cases in Massachusetts were receiving widespread publicity.

As a result of these and many other examples of increasing public awareness and concern, H.R. 25 was subjected to lengthy and critical evaluation. The hearings before the House Subcommittee on Fisheries and Wildlife Conservation resulted in a 486-page publication, <u>Estuarine Areas</u>, which continues to provide valuable insight into the positions of most of the players in the Coastal Zone management game.[1] H.R. 25 failed to provide a management system. It passed the Congress but was weakened to the point of virtual impotency. The deliberations surrounding it, both within Washington and without, did, however, provide the foundation from which systems now under consideration evolved.

At about the same time that Congressman Dingell's first bill failed to pass, the Congress passed the Clean Water Restoration Act (P.L. 89-753), directed toward improving the national water-pollution control program. One section of this bill--Section 5(g)-- directed the Secretary of the Interior to prepare recommendations for a comprehensive national program for the preservation, study, use, and development of estuaries of the nation and respective responsibilities that should be assumed by federal, state, and local governments and by private interests--in essence, a Coastal Zone management program--by November 3, 1969.

Involved in the area of these developments in the Congress and the Department of the Interior is the work of the National Commission on Marine Resources and Engineering Development, a Presidentially appointed body charged with recommending an over-all plan for an adequate national oceanographic program, and the National Council on Marine Resources and Engineering Development, which assists the President in developing and coordinating federal marine-science activities. The Commission recommended a system of Coastal Zone management in which primary responsibility was vested in the states, with federal legislation to encourage and support state Coastal Zone authorities to carry out specified national objectives. The Council's Committee on Multiple Use of the Coastal Zone and subsequent Task Force on Coastal Zone Authorities recommended enactment of a Coastal Zone management system. In October, 1969, Vice-President Spiro Agnew announced administration support for a five-point national marine-science program, one element of which was a Coastal Zone management program.

The brief history outlined above illustrates the following points: (a) comprehensive natural-resource management in the Coastal Zone is a relatively new concept in government; (b) the individual states, the Congress, and several agencies in the executive branch of the federal government have been working along more or less parallel paths toward an acceptable system; and (c) public support for some more adequate mechanism to manage the environment, particularly the coastal environment, has increased and intensified tremendously in recent years and is continuing to do so.

BILLS BEFORE THE 91st CONGRESS

Unfortunately, the parallel paths have not converged to a single one and enactment of a national Coastal Zone management program is not imminent.

FEDERAL-STATE MANAGEMENT SYSTEMS 23

Bills based upon the Commission's recommendations and vesting federal jurisdiction in the Marine Sciences Council (H.R. 15099 and S. 2802) or the proposed National Oceanographic and Atmospheric Agency (H.R. 14730) were pending in the 91st Congress. Administration-sponsored bills based on the Federal Water Quality Adminstration Report and vesting jurisdiction in the Environmental Protection Agency were also presented to the 91st Congress, as were at least three similar bills (H.R. 14731, H.R. 16155, and S. 3460).

In toto, this legislation invloves three existing executive agencies (Environmental Protection Agency, Marine Sciences Council, and National Oceanographic and Atmospheric Agency), two committees of the House of Representatives (Public Works and Merchant Marine and Fisheries), and two committees of the Senate (Public Works and Commerce). Despite these complexities (and they are serious ones), all of the bills contain the same general provisions, and any one of them could provide a workable basis for a national Coastal Zone management program (for, regardless of what is enacted, subsequent events will dictate modifications and revisions). In order to simplify this discussion, a detailed analysis of all these various versions will not be given; instead, the administration proposal will be used as an example, citing other versions only when necessary for comparison.

FEATURES OF THE ADMINISTRATION PROPOSAL

H.R. 14845 begins with a declaration of national interest in effective management, beneficial use, protection, and development of the land and water resources of the nation's estuaries and Coastal Zone. It recognizes the value of estuaries and marshland as habitats for interstate populations of fish and wildlife and the increasing and diverse demands to which they are being subjected and notes that such areas constitute ecological systems that are susceptible to destruction and disruption by man. The policy statements further declare that continued unplanned and uncoordinated development pose an immediate threat of irreversible harm to the Coastal Zone, within which the citizens of all the states have an interest.

These policy statements serve an important function in addition to being a fitting introduction to the act. They provide the basis for national (i.e., federal) involvement in Coastal Zone resources management and elucidate the nature of the public interest involved. States attempting to develop their own management systems should take note of this latter function and pay particular attention to policy declarations within their legislation, for the outcome of subsequent litigation testing the validity of their systems may depend upon an adequate declaration of legislative intent and definition of the public trust.

The provisions of the bill apply to all coastal states and, more specifically, to the Coastal Zone within such states. Many have attempted to define Coastal Zone, but no one has really been successful in doing so. The basic problem is one of separating one part of a continuum--from the ocean to the mountains--in such a way that that part, the Coastal Zone, is a natural and easily defined entity. To do so is impossible, but some geographical description is necessary. Here, the Congress is defining the Coastal Zone for the purpose of a federal-state management system in which primary authority is vested in the individual states. Obviously, the outer limit of such an area cannot exceed the offshore limit of state jurisdiction, but the internal limit becomes somewhat subjective, based more on political considerations than on geographic ones.

In this bill, Coastal Zone means the "land, waters, and lands beneath the waters in close proximity to the coastline . . . and strongly influenced by each other . . . [and] extends seaward to the outer limits of the United States territorial sea." Subsequent provisions require the states to identify the boundaries of their Coastal Zone more precisely, but the basis for such boundary determination is

FEDERAL-STATE MANAGEMENT SYSTEMS   25

left to the individual states. In comparison, S.
3460 provides that the Coastal Zone not exceed twenty
miles in width, and S. 2802 defines the inland boundary as the "landward extent of maritime influences."

   The proposed federal grant program is to be
provided in two phases: program development and
operation. In the first phase, states are eligible
for 50 per cent federal funding up to a maximum of
$200,000 per year to develop comprehensive Coastal
Zone management programs. No time period is specified, but the Secretary of the Interior may refuse
to make subsequent annual grants if he feels the
state is not adequately and expeditiously developing
its program. States become eligible for operating
grants (not to exceed 50 per cent of the total cost,
but no more than $200,000 per year) upon review and
approval of their plan by the Secretary of the Interior. Criteria for approval are spelled out in
considerable detail, and states should give serious
consideration to these criteria in any Coastal Zone
management plan under development.

   According to H.R. 14845, the Secretary of the
Interior must find that (a) the governor has designated
a single agency to receive and administer operating
grants and has approved the management plan; (b) the
state is organized to implement the plan; (c) responsible state agencies have sufficient regulatory
authority for implementation, including permit authority, authority to acquire interest in real property
through the power of eminent domain, and zone authority
or authority to require local zoning to conform with
the state plan; (d) adequate public notice and public
hearings were provided during the development of the
plan; and (e) the state plan contains the following
elements:

   1. an identification of the area subject
      to the management plan

   2. an identification and recognition of
      national, state, and local interests

   3. a feasible land- and water-use plan

reflecting the needs of all interests and taking into account both short-term and long-term requirements

4. a description of the state's current and planned management programs

5. an identification of the plan's relationship to state, interstate, and regional planning and the means by which coordination will be effected among all levels of government

6. procedures for reviewing state, local, and private projects for consistency with the management plan and for furnishing advice as to the relationship of federal and federally assisted projects to the plan

7. procedures for regular revision, modification, and change, including public notice and hearings

8. evidence that the plan was developed in cooperation with all relevant interests, including federal, state, and local government

9. adequate provisions for disseminating information concerning the plan

10. provisions for conducting, fostering, or utilizing relevant research.

These provisions were based on three underlying principles: (a) the federal government should not fund an operation that is doomed to failure because it lacks the capability to perform the task assigned, (b) the states should have maximum latitude to develop programs to meet the special requirements of their areas, and (c) the public should be aware of the planning process and have ample opportunity to review and contribute to the plan as it develops.

FEDERAL-STATE MANAGEMENT SYSTEMS 27

In this case, the single-agency requirement facilitates liaison between state and federal government but does not foreclose the possibility that a number of state agencies might be involved in the actual management operation. The permit-authority, eminent-domain, and zoning requirements assure that the state has the capability to implement its plan. Zoning is a particularly sensitive part of the Coastal Zone management concept, and many local governments and special districts may view this provision with considerable alarm.

H.R. 14845 does not *require* land-use zoning at the state level, but it does require that the state must be able to require local zoning to conform with the state management plan. S. 2802 and S. 3460 contain a stronger suggestion of zoning by a state agency, and H.R. 14731 requires either state-agency zoning authority or state authority to override local zoning inconsistent with the state management plan. Hopefully, these requirements may be met through tactful negotiation and accommodation and judicious use of the state permit authority without necessarily pre-empting the zoning authority now vested in county and municipal governments.

The drafters of this legislation paid particular attention to the necessity for public involvement. Public notice and hearings are required in the initial plan development and in any modification of the plan. These are important provisions, for the courts are taking an increasingly dim view of governmental policy, and particularly governmental regulation, developed without public involvement. Anyone working on state plans should be sure that all interests have been contacted and considered--a frustrating, but necessary, process.

The pending legislation varies considerably with respect to the one-phase versus two-phase aspect. A single-phase program--that is, one grant for planning and implementation--might be simplest to administer. A two-phase program provides an opportunity to evaluate the state plan before implementation grants are awarded. If too inflexible, however, states might be denied operating funds for portions of their Coastal Zone for which an adequate plan had been developed until such time as the entire state plan was completed.

H.R. 14730 describes a one-phase program; S. 2802 and S. 3460 provide that the state plan may be adopted in segments; and H.R. 14845 specifies that a state must have a feasible land- and water-use plan within specified sections of the Coastal Zone in order to qualify for operating grants. These last provisions sufficiently confound the matter as to place discretionary authority in the Secretary of the Interior to determine when a state passes from program development to the operational stage. Whether or not a state can continue to receive up to $200,000 per year in program-development grants for a part of its work at the same time that it receives up to $200,000 per year for implementation is not entirely clear and could result in states' concentrating their efforts on an unreasonably small coastal area in order to gain approval for that part of their plan and to receive additional funds.

THE COORDINATION PROBLEM

The problem of coordination will be one of the most severe faced by both federal and state agencies administering Coastal Zone programs. A number of studies have attempted to list all governmental bodies operating in the Coastal Zone and to define the extent of their interests. The answer is always the same; everyone is playing around, and who is left off and who is put on such a list is entirely arbitrary. Developing a scheme that will meet the coordination requirements of these bills, not conflict with other federal requirements (such as those already existing under the Intergovernmental Cooperation Act of 1968 and the Water Resources Planning Act), and still mesh efficiently with the diverse forms of government existing in the respective states will be a monumental task.

At least part of the coordination scheme is

written into the bill. The Department of the Interior and other federal agencies are afforded opportunities to influence the state plan at three stages: (a) they will be involved in plan formulation, (b) they will assist in developing rules and regulations covering the submission and review of grant applications, and (c) they will assist the Secretary of the Interior in the approval process. H.R. 14845 contains some very interesting language on this last aspect. It states that "The Secretary shall not approve the plan . . . until he has solicited the views of Federal agencies principally affected by such plan or his [sic] evidence that the views were provided the State in the development of the plan."

Initial considerations of Coastal Zone management recognized the necessity for a federal review of state programs but gave little consideration to the necessity for involving federal agencies in plan formulation. The above wording seems to be an additional encouragement for the state to solicit early federal involvement and to imply that such involvement might minimize the federal critique at the Secretary of the Interior level.

The administration bill authorizes the Secretary of the Interior to establish advisory committees to assist him in policy matters concerning the Coastal Zone. The number of such committees and their composition is not specified, nor is the Secretary of the Interior required to establish them. It would appear to the states' interest to require the creation and utilization of at least one advisory committee and to insist upon adequate state representation on it.

THE ROLE OF FEDERAL AGENCIES

One important and far-reaching provision concerns the relationship of federal projects to the state plan. H.R. 14845 requires that federal agencies "should seek to make such activities consistent with the approved plan" and "shall not approve proposed projects that are inconsistent with the plan without making investigation and finding that the proposed project is, on balance, sound." S. 2802 deviates somewhat, prohibiting federal agencies from undertaking a project inconsistent with the plan unless detailed comments are received from both the federal agency and Coastal Zone authorities and unless the Marine Sciences Council "finds that such project is, on balance, consistent with the general objectives of this title." H.R. 14730 and H.R. 14731 do not address this issue, and S. 3460 requires federal agencies to consult with the coastal authorities prior to conducting activities in the Coastal Zone, in addition to containing the provisions of S. 2802.

Just as the state-county relationship in zoning was a sensitive issue, the degree to which federal activities will be made subject to state Coastal Zone planning is also a very delicate matter. One can readily appreciate the hesitancy with which federal agencies conducting strong programs with their constituent groups at the state and local levels would embrace this concept. Their reticence may be even more marked in view of a preface policy statement that "priority should be given to preserving non-renewable resources" (S. 3460).

PROSPECTS FOR ENACTMENT

At the present time, it is impossible to tell which, if any, of the proposed Coastal Zone bills will pass the Congress. It is certain, however, that any bill that does pass will contain the following provisions:

1. That financial assistance be given to the states for the development and implementation of Coastal Zone management programs

2. That a single agency be designated as a state contact for the federal agency administering the program, but considerable latitude for the states to develop their own internal organization

FEDERAL-STATE MANAGEMENT SYSTEMS

3. That the states possess the capability both to develop the plan and to implement it

4. That the state plan be truly comprehensive, taking into account all interests and all levels of government

5. That adequate opportunity for public involvement be afforded

6. That federal agencies be given an opportunity to contribute to state planning efforts

7. That the management program be linked with the state's research activities.

All of the bills which have been proposed contained the above elements to a greater or lesser degree. Any of them could do the job, if efficiently administered; but there is a chance that events will overtake this whole concept of Coastal Zone management while committees of the Congress and executive agencies are bogged down in jurisdictional disputes and opponents of the bill are sniping away at petty differences in wording.

On January 29, 1970, Senator Henry M. Jackson of the state of Washington introduced a bill (S. 3354) to amend the Water Resources Planning Act to include provisions for a national land-use policy by broadening the authority of the Water Resources Council and River Basin Commissions and by providing financial assistance for state-wide land-use planning. In essence, this bill applies the concepts developed in considerations of Coastal Zone management to the land and water resources of the entire nation. If enacted, it would pre-empt all Coastal Zone legislation now pending. The possibility of its enactment might, however, slow down the consideration of Coastal Zone legislation or stir up such a fracas that any scheme for comprehensive natural-resource management might be defeated.

NOTE

1. U.S. Congress, House Committee on Merchant Marine and Fisheries, <u>Estuarine Areas, Hearings</u>, before the Subcommittee on Fisheries and Wildlife Conversation of the Committee on Merchant Marine and Fisheries, House of Representatives, on H.R. 25, 90th Cong., 1st sess., Serial No. 90-3, 1967.

CHAPTER

3

**MANAGEMENT SYSTEMS
UNDER CONSIDERATION
AT THE STATE-LOCAL LEVEL:
THE SOUTH ATLANTIC COAST**

by Frederick C. Marland

FEDERAL EFFORTS AND SCOPE OF THE PROBLEM

On August 3, 1968, President Lyndon Johnson signed a much weakened H.R. 25 bill into law (P.L. 90-454). The original intent of the bill as introduced by Congressman Herbert Tenzer of New York (H.R. 1397 [89th Congress]), Congressman John D. Dingell of Michigan (H.R. 25 [90th Congress]), and others was to develop a wise and operational management system for the nation's estuaries. The testimony offered reveals that the bill was weakened by the Army Corps of Engineers, several public officials pleading states' rights, and many people who are unaware of the relative value of a natural estuary versus an artificial estuary.[1] The most needed section of the bill, a permit system for dredging and filling, was not enacted. Instead, the main feature of the law is nearly identical to a section of the Clean Water Restoration Act of 1966, which provides for the Secretary of the Interior to study and assembly information on the nation's estuaries and report recommendations to the Congress.[2]

The most important estuarine recommendation concerns their protection and wise use, through an intergovernmental permit system to control dredging and filling in estuaries and on water bottoms. This concern was well summarized by S. Fred Singer:

> It will probably take many years before a national management system for estuaries is worked out, converted into legislation, and put into operation throughout our nation. . . . The need, as I see it, expressed in sharply drawn terms, is to make sure that there are estuaries left to manage when a national management system is finally adopted.[3]

The national interest was not served by the deletion of Section 12 of H.R. 25, which thwarted the attempt to get a meaningful dredging and filling permit system. The obliteration of the estuarine landscape continues at an increasing pace, despite new state laws and imaginative legal action.

Because of compartmentalized governmental systems, it is difficult to cope with the problems of stewardship of the estuarine zone. Existing structures and political arrangements for the Coastal Zone are inadequate for wise management. The problem of management in the U.S. Coastal Zone becomes evident when one realizes just what the area defined includes:

1. All or portions of thirty states and the District of Columbia

2. 413 counties, including several cities that operate independently of counties

3. A land surface of 424,156 square miles (exclusive of continental shelf or water surface to the territorial limits of the United States)

4. A population in 1960 of 78,345,527.[4]

David A. Adams has considered the strengths and weaknesses of each level (local, state, regional, and federal) of government for improved management of the Coastal Zone.[5] The fragmented governmental jurisdictions cannot be easily transferred from high and fast land across the shoreline into the intertidal and marine zone. It is the view of Alfred A. Porro, Jr., that the federal government should encourage the establishment of state Coastal Zone authorities only with the proviso that the states' participation be mandatory and that no new agencies be created. Porro also notes the lack of coordination, the ineffectiveness, and the illegality of various states' approaches to the problem.[6]

LEGALISMS AND A NEW PHILOSOPHY OF LAW

In the southeastern United States, the marshes are of such character concerning use and future development, particularly when the tide is in, as to require separate consideration from the high land. Georgia Attorney General Arthur K. Bolton has ruled that the marshlands of Georgia are not susceptible to private exploitation or conservation without regard to the common-law trust purposes to which these lands have long been dedicated.[7] This is also made clear in the recent opinion of the Supreme Court of the state of Washington (No. 39444), in William L. Griffin's white paper on the legal bases of state Coastal Zone regulation, and in Aaron L. Shalowitz' treatise on shore and sea boundaries.[8] Such land and the waters that cover them, either part or all of the time, have been treated by Anglo-American law as a common property resource.

This land has been incapable of ordinary and private occupation and of other traditional uses of land but has served as a thoroughfare and haven for marine biota and a place of recreation for the citizenry. The elements and consequences of title are thus qualified by the public right to use such tidal waters and the lands thereby covered, but, unfortunately, the laws of most of the southeastern states are neither fully formulated nor precisely drawn to meet the demands of the present day.[9]

Time is needed to implement the new philosophy of the law that is emerging. This new ethic for the land is inherent in the interrelatedness of the ecosystem and is based on a changing concept of the public interest. The ethic is best expressed in the notion that property rights do not necessarily mean profit rights. This is not alien doctrine. Its roots are firmly based in Anglo-American law. This new ethic is made apparent by the "tragedy of the commons." As Garrett Hardin points out:

> The tragedy of the commons as a food basket is averted by private property. Indeed, our particular concept of private property, which deters us from exhausting the positive resourses of the earth, favors pollution . . . But <u>air and water surrounding us cannot readily be fenced</u>, and so the tragedy of the commons as a cesspool must be prevented by different means, by coercive laws or taxing devices that make it cheaper for the polluter to treat his pollutants than to discharge them untreated.[10]

Victor John Yannacone, Jr., expressed the new jurisprudence when he said: "Let each man and every corporation so use his property as not to injure that of another, particularly so as not to injure that which is common property of all the people."[11]

The traditional concept of the marshes, the sounds, the beaches, and the nearshore environment as a common is now threatened. The Coastal Zone is being fenced, diked, filled, leased, and sold upon assumptions not founded on clear legality. For example, a complaint was filed in the Federal District Court in New Jersey by Alfred A. Porro, Jr., against the state in an attempt to stop a sale of marshland to the Central Railroad. The property was sold for $16,000 by the state and resold the same day for $710,000.

THE GEORGIA EXPERIENCE

As pointed out by E. P. Odum in his testimony in support of Georgia's Coastal Marshlands Protection Act, there are bigger reasons other than ownership why the marshes should be conserved. Until recently, man has more or less taken for granted the gas exchange, water purification, nutrient cycling, buffering of storm tides, and other protective functions of a self-maintaining unit of the landscape such as a marsh ecosystem.

In March, 1970, Governor Lester Maddox of Georgia signed into law the Coastal Marshlands Protection Act, which culminated a two-year struggle by many legislators, citizens, conversation groups, public officials, and scientists to have the state of Georgia and the legislature assert its responsibility for the stewardship of one of its natural resources.[12] As one speaker said, these salt marsh prairies are Georgia's Grand Canyon. That the marshlands bill was successful was mainly an affirmation of the courage and statesmanship of its principal author, State Representative Reid W. Harris. He sacrificed much. From time to time, the Brunswick lawyer and legislator ushered former clients or old political supporters into his office, only to hear that friend inform him that, henceforth, his support would go elsewhere.[13]

Those opposed to the bill included members of the local chamber of commerce, the mayor of Brunswick, the city manager, Glynn County Commissioners and officials, the two major industries (a pulp mill and a chemical plant), labor-union officials, and the Sea Island Company (a recreation and development company). The opposition to the state-wide bill had maintained that the local planning authority was sufficient to regulate the use of the marshlands. In two of the five public hearings held on this legislation, Hoyt Brown of the Marshes of Glynn Association made a case-history study with maps and documents to show that the local zoning and planning boards had not measured up.

As the law is implemented in the state and becomes more widely known in the nation, it will hopefully be recognized that the legislative process did rearrange its evaluation of what constitutes a resource. That rearrangement was led by State Senator Al Holloway, Chairman of the Industry and Labor Committee and President of the State Chamber of Commerce.

THE SOUTH CAROLINA CONTROVERSY

Edward B. Latimer has raised the question of whether the states can sell tidelands.[14] At the time, in 1968, the South Carolina Attorney General's Office took the position that the state held these lands in trust and could not sell these areas. In 1969, South Carolina laid claim to the tidelands, except those tidelands previously granted by the Lord Proprietors, the Crown, or by previous grant from the state.[15] This restatement of the state's sovereignty to all tidelands differs from Latimer since management, development, navigation, and commerce are now stressed as probable uses of these trust lands.[16]

In the 1970 South Carolina controversy, concerning Badische Anilin and Soda Fabrik Company (BASF), no tidelands were conveyed to the Company. Among the inducements that South Carolina offered BASF were the following: the Port Authority sold 1,800 acres of land at about one-fifth the real value as part of the plant site; South Carolina further promised two state docks for handling bulk cargo and for liquid handling of oil and naptha, a railroad spur to the property, a new highway to the plant, and a five-year moratorium on county taxes except for school taxes.

A German scientist who is familiar with the BASF plant at Ludwigshafen-on-the-Rhine suggested that, with the toughening of controls, the company had now turned its interests to the coasts of northern Europe because "there are no rules." Prior to the recent controversy, ecological surveys, and litigation,

STATE-LOCAL MANAGEMENT SYSTEMS 39

the weak pollution laws and enforcement in South Carolina were apparently a strong inducement.[17] There is ample evidence that the pollution control agencies to the north and south are much more stringent.

ARMY CORPS OF ENGINEERS PERMIT SYSTEM

Historically, most shoreline and port developments have been accomplished by dredging and filling the estuarine zone. This constitutes one of the most controversial issues today, and it is perhaps the most severe problem for the future.[18] One exercise of the federal power over navigation is implemented by the River and Harbor Act of 1899.[19] At present, this act is administered by the Army Corps of Engineers and, among other things, provides for the authorization by permit of dredging and filling in navigable waters. It is a premise of this paper that the dredging and filling permit system administered by the Army Corps of Engineers and implemented in Georgia and other states is inadequate to deal with the wanton destruction of the estuarine zone. Moreover, there are two federal district court cases that call to question the statutory authority of the Corps to issue permits.

Until 1968, the Corps acted merely as a licensing bureau for those who made application. It is policy that permit applications are not denied but merely held in abeyance.[20] Different district permit officers have told the author this. In fact, nowhere in the Corps pamphlet on permit applications is the word denial used or the suggestion made that some permit applications might be turned down.[21] If the permit draws objections from citizens, the applicant reads each criticism and submits a modified plan.[22]

During this process, the Corps is noncommittal to citizen requests as to the handling and status of the permit. When things have quieted down, the Corps usually grants the permit without public disclosure. This is doubly true concerning federally sponsored dredging and engineering projects. The state, local government, or citizen has little advanced engineering information at hand to evaluate these large-scale engineering plans. A Corps project to build a number of dams on the upper Potomac and its tributaries was, however, recently challenged by economists at Resources for the Future.[23]

It should be noted that the Department of the Interior processes approximately 6,000 permit referrals from the Corps each year.[24] Many of these are routine. On the more controversial ones, however, the Corps in the last several years denied less than 1 per cent of the applications.[25] Testimony developed by Congressman Henry S. Reuss of Wisconsin indicates that the Army-Department of the Interior dredging agreement based on the 1967 Memorandum of Understanding raises a number of serious questions.[26] Not the least of these is the abhorrence of the Corps to protecting the public interest and using the courts to prosecute violators.

When illegal dredging on a 1,200-acre dike project began in McIntosh County, Georgia, without a permit, it was difficult to get the Corps to order a halt.[27] The potential violator was warned, in one Corps release, that "Failure to obtain the necessary permit is a violation of the Laws of the United States and can result in legal complications." [Emphasis added.] Another difficulty is that two major coastal engineering firms in Savannah either employ or are managed by retired Corps district engineers.

One of the few permits to be denied by the Corps was a land-fill project in Boca Ciega Bay, Florida. This permit was denied for reasons other than adverse effects upon navigation.[28] The dredging was opposed by federal, state, and local agencies including the County Commissioners. At issue in this first test case is the ability of the Corps to deny a dredging and filling permit for reasons other than navigability.[29] The district court ruled that the U.S. Fish and Wildlife Coordination Act does not vest the Secretary of the Army with discretionary authority to deny an application that would not interfere with navigation. The court directed the Corps to issue the permit. The case is now on appeal before the Fifth Circuit Court, New Orleans (filed December, 1969). A three-judge panel of the Fifth Circuit Court of Appeals heard arguments in Jacksonville, Florida, in January, 1970, and reversed the lower court.

In the four actions challenging the construction of the proposed six-lane Hudson River expressway, the plaintiff's major claim was that, since the project involved dikes, causeways, and bridges to be built over or in a navigable waterway of the United States, the Corps exceeded its statutory authority in issuing the permit without the prior approval of Congress as required by 33 U.S.C. sec. 401 of the River and Harbor Act of 1899. The U.S. District Court, Southern District of New York, found that the Corps had exceeded its authority.

Since this case, the Corps is still in the business of issuing permits but with a new set of semantics. For example, the new Public Notices of permit applications (e.g., SASKS-WW 3083, May 8, 1970, concerning a causeway to Green Island) substitute the word "roadway" for "causeway," the word "berm" replaces "dike," and the word "bridge" is not used. Comments are not asked for on the reduction in width of a navigable river from 390 to 30 feet. The Corps evidently plans to issue permits not based on fish and wildlife or on navigation questions but on the strength of its organization.

Many question why the Department of Defense--specifically, the Army Corps of Engineers--is engaged in damming streams and rivers and filling in estuarine areas in the name of such activities as ecology, navigation, water supply, flood control, water quality, and recreation. With the current expenditure by the Department of Defense of some $80 billion per year, it is inevitable that many massive engineering projects would include the estuaries. The country's national defense and navigational interests do not require that much participation in the Coastal Zones. There are those who would reform the Corps and give them much greater responsibility in environmental management.[30] It is this author's view that there are too few rivers, waterways, or undamaged landscapes for that luxury. Critics of the Corps charge the agency with bureaucratic highhandedness and assert that many of its expensive projects are economically unjustified.[31] It is necessary, instead, to replace the civil works of the Corps with a truly civilian environmental engineering agency. Multidisciplined teams of people and systems analysis could cope with environmental problems if they were properly mobilized.

SUMMARY

The Corps does not concern itself with ecology, aesthetics, site modification, nor even the social or economic impact of the filling projects that it licenses. To be quite candid, and despite Corps pleading to the contrary, the Corps' outlook is much too limited to develop a sound operational policy of Coastal Zone resources. The question is: When a district Corps office grants a permit to fill and thereby destroy irreversibly one acre of marshland, does the Army have any idea of the long-range economic and human benefits that have been foreclosed? This myopia applies equally well to scientists and engineers. The state and nation are being called upon to register the nonmarket values and to develop wise management policies of the Coastal Zone. This can be done only when more states enact Coastal Zone legislation consistent with their different ecological settings and legislative and court histories.

In the interim, the Congress must enact a new dredging and filling permit law, since many states lack such a law. Moreover, the Corps lacks statutory authority to issue permits as provided in the River and Harbor Act of 1899. In a new federal law, the decision-makers and the final deliberations on permits should be made more open to public scrutiny. The Departments of Commerce and the Interior should play a dual role in administering this new law.

NOTES

1. U.S. Congress, House Committee on Merchant Marine and Fisheries, Estuarine Areas, Hearings, before the Subcommittee on Fisheries and Wildlife Conservation of the Committee on Merchant Marine and Fisheries, House of Representatives, on H.R. 25, 90th Cong., 1st sess., Serial No. 90-3, p. 486, 1967. (Edward A. Garmatz, Chairman).

2. U.S. Department of the Interior, Federal Water Pollution Control Administration (report to Congress), "The National Estuarine Pollution Study" (3 vols.; Washington, D.C., 1969). (Mimeographed.)

3. S. Fred Singer, "The Federal Interest in Estuaries" (remarks before the Oyster Institute of North America, Washington, D.C., 1968).

4. Harold F. Wise and Associates, "Intergovernmental Relations and the National Interest in the Coastal Zone of the United States," Document No. PB 184 212 (Springfield, Va.: Clearinghouse for Federal Scientific and Technical Information, 1969).

5. David A. Adams, "Proposals for Improved Coastal Zone Management Systems" (Seminar on Multiple Use of the Coastal Zone, National Council on Marine Resources and Engineering Development, Williamsburg Va., 1968), pp. 124-39.

6. Alfred A. Porro, Jr., "The Coastal and Estuarine Zone: A National Interest" (statement to the Subcommittee on Oceanography of the Committee on Merchant Marine and Fisheries, U.S. House of Representatives, Washington, D.C., October 28 and 29, 1969). (Mimeographed.)

7. Arthur W. Bolton and Courtney Stanton, "Legal Ramifications of Various Applications and Proposals Relative to the Development of Georgia's Coastal Marshes" (white paper, ruling by Attorney General of Georgia, Atlanta, Ga., 1970).

8. See William L. Griffin, "Legal Bases of State Coastal Zone Regulation" (paper presented at Institute of Ocean Law, University of Miami, Miami, Fla., December 10-12, 1969); and Aaron L. Shalowitz, Shore and Sea Boundaries, with Special Reference to the Interpretation and Use of Coast and Geodetic Survey Data (2 vols.; Washington, D.C.: U.S. Government Printing Office, 1962-64).

9. See Milton S. Heath, Jr., State Programs for Estuarine Area Conservation (Chapel Hill, N.C.: University of North Carolina at Chapel Hill, Institute of Government, 1968); Edward B. Latimer, "Jurisdiction and Ownership of Marshes and Estuaries of the South Atlantic and Gulf Coasts," in J. D. Newsom, ed., Proceedings, Marsh and Estuary Management Symposium (Baton Rough: Louisiana State University, 1968, pp. 33-40; and Maurice P. Lynch, "Legal Aspects of Wetlands," in M. L. Wass and T. D. Wright, eds., Coastal Wetlands of Virginia, "Special Report in Applied Science and Ocean Engineering," No. 10 (Gloucester Point, Va: Virginia Institute of Marine Science, 1969), pp. 97-113.

10. Garrett Hardin, "The Tragedy of the Commons," Science, Vol. 162 (1968), pp. 1,243-48.

11. Victor John Yannacone, Jr., "A Lawyer Answers the Technocrats," Trial Magazine (August-September, 1969), pp. 14-15.

12. Reid W. Harris et al., Coastal Marshlands Protection Act (State Senate substitute for H.B. 212), 1970, is available at the Clerk's Office, 309 State Capitol, Atlanta, Georgia.

13. Jeff Nesmith, "The Salt Marshes--Threatened World; Part 1, Tide of Abuse Hits Conservation," Atlanta Journal and Constitution, November 2, 1969.

14. Latimer, op. cit., p. 37.

15. Clair P. Guess, Jr., et al., South Carolina Tidelands Report (Columbia, S.C.: South Carolina Water Resources Commission, 1969).

STATE-LOCAL MANAGEMENT SYSTEMS   45

16. See Latimer, op. cit.

17. Clair P. Guess, Jr., "South Carolina Estuarine Environmental Studies, Step 1--A Profile of a Proposed Environmental Analysis of Port Royal Sound, Colleton River, Victoria Bluff, Beaufort, S.C." (Columbia, S.C.: South Carolina Water Resources Commission, March 18, 1970). (Mimeographed.)

18. John Knauss, ed., Science and Environment; Industry and Technology; Marine Resources and Legal-Political Arrangements for Their Development (panel reports of the Commission on Marine Science, Engineering and Resources), Vol. 1 (Washington, D.C., 1969), p. 36.

19. River and Harbor Act of March 3, 1899; 30 STAT. 1151; as amended, 33 U.S.C. Secs. 401-416 (1964).

20. Letter of Major General F. J. Clarke, Deputy Chief of Engineers, to Congressman Henry S. Reuss, in U.S., Congress, House, Committee on Government Operations, The Nation's Estuaries: San Francisco Bay and Delta, California, Hearings, before the Subcommittee on Conservation and Natural Resources of the Committee on Government Operations (Washington, D.C., 1970), Part 2, pp. 554-55.

21. U.S. Department of the Army, Corps of Engineers, Permits for Work in Navigable Waters (1968).

22. Clarke, op. cit., p. 555.

23. McGeorge Bundy, Managing Knowledge to Save the Environment (New York: The Ford Foundation, 1970), p. 8.

24. Russell E. Train, in The Nation's Estuaries, Part 2, p. 445.

25. U.S. Congress, House Committee on Merchant Marine and fisheries, Estuarine Areas, op. cit., p. 129. (Testimony of Alfred B. Fitt)

26. See The Nation's Estuaries, Parts 1-2.

27. U.S. Congress, House Committee on Merchant Marine and Fisheries, Estuarine Areas, op. cit., p. 100. (Testimony of Alfred B. Fitt).

28. Knauss, op. cit., p. 131.

29. Zabel v. Tabb, Alfred G. Zabel and David H. Russell, Plaintiffs, v. R. H. Tabb, Colonel, Corps of Engineers, and Stanley R. Resor, Secretary of the Army, and the United States of America, in U.S. District Court for Middle District of Florida, Tampa Division No. 67-200 Civ. T.

30. John Cairns, Jr., and P. S. Humphrey, A Water Resources Ecology Capability for the Waterways Experiment Station and Corps of Engineers (contract report for Corps)(Vicksburg, Miss., 1969).

31. Tom Herman, "Embattled Corps--Army Engineers Draw Increasing Critical Fire for Disturbing Nature," Wall Street Journal, January 6, 1970.

PART II
POLICY CONSIDERATIONS

CHAPTER

4

LEGAL
AND
INSTITUTIONAL
CONSIDERATIONS

by Milton S. Heath, Jr.

By way of introduction, it will be useful to review briefly the current institutional and organizational setting regarding legal and institutional considerations in the management of coastal resources --in Washington, in the states, and at the local or regional level.

THE FEDERAL SETTING

As David A. Adams has noted in chapter 2, above, there is, in fact, nothing in existence that merits the name of a management system at the federal level. There was perhaps the making of a management system in the 1967 bill of Congressman John D. Dingell of Michigan (H.R. 25 [90th Congress]) as originally conceived by its introducer. The federalist spirit of this proposal has not yet prevailed, however, nor is its star currently in the ascendancy.

During the past several years, there has been a broadly conceived federal study machinery in operation seeking management solutions--that is, the National Council on Marine Resources and Engineering Development and the Commission on Marine Science, Engineering, and Resources. Out of this study effort has emerged an apparent thrust towards a management system that focuses responsibility and action on the states, stimulated by federal grants and somewhat circumscribed by federal criteria. As Adams has pointed out, the prospects of this movement are tied to the fate of several bills now competing for approval of the Congress, and it is impossible to predict when new federal legislation is likely to be enacted. Washington Senator Henry M. Jackson's recently introduced all-embracing bill (S. 3354) provides for a national land-use policy and has introduced new elements of unpredictability into the timetable for federal Coastal Zone legislation.

Finally, it should be noted that there are some existing tools for federal management, primarily the Army Corps of Engineers permits, concerning work that will affect "navigable waters." Several years ago, an adverse federal district court decision dimmed the prospects for using this permit mechanism as a means of evaluating the environmental impact of alterations in and around estuarine waters. The enactment of the National Environmental Policy Act of 1969--with its clear mandate that all federal agencies take into account the environmental impact of their programs and actions--has apparently breathed new life into the Corps' permit proceedings, however.

On May 19, 1970, the Corps announced what it termed "sweeping changes" in its regulations pertaining to work in navigable waterways. Under the new regulations, the basis for consideration of permit applications will again be broadened to include fish and wildlife, water quality, conservation, aesthetic, recreation, water supply, flood-damage prevention, ecosystems, and in general, "the needs and welfare to the people." (See Appendix A, below, for the text of the Corps' news release.)

THE STATE SETTING

In Chapter 3, above, Frederick C. Marland discussed management system being evolved in the state of Georgia. If one looks to other coastal

LEGAL AND INSTITUTIONAL CONSIDERATIONS

states, several developing patterns can be found, thus far geared mainly to estuaries rather than to the entire Coastal Zone. Something resembling the Georgia regulatory approach is being evolved in at least six coastal states--North Carolina and the five New England states (Connecticut, Maine, Massachusetts, New Hampshire, and Rhode Island). One of these five, Massachusetts, has taken the significant further step of authorizing a rule-making approach (that is, the adopting of regulations to control the alteration of wetlands on a regional basis) in addition to case-by-case permit controls.

Estuarine land acquisition is a significant element in several states--New Jersey, North Carolina, California, Maine, Connecticut, Rhode Island, and Delaware. The ultimate power of condemnation is available in about half of these states. State acquisition is often supplemented by acquisition efforts to private conservation groups and federal agencies.

A coordinated state plan of regulation and acquisition is well illustrated by Florida's recently initiated state-wide system of aquatic preserves. The aquatic-preserve concept assumes that some of Florida's coastal areas are of special value to the state in their natural condition and should be dedicated and managed in perpetuity as protected aquatic preserves. An aquatic preserves will be one or a combination of three types--biological (to preserve or promote certain forms of animal or plant life), aesthetic (to preserve scenic qualities or amenities), or scientific (to preserve certain features, qualities, or conditions for scientific or educational purposes). In these preserves, of which twenty-five are projected, no additional state-owned submerged lands would be sold, and no dredging or filling permits to create waterfront real estate would be issued.

A program of state-local cooperation has been pioneered in New York under the Long Island Wetlands Act. This provides for state-local cost-sharing in maintenance and operation of locally owned wetlands

that have been dedicated for conservation purposes.
The possible use of gubernatorial powers to temporarily hold the line while state planning efforts
are in process has been illustrated by an Executive
Order issued in March, 1970, by the governor of
Oregon, temporarily restraining state construction
agencies from pursuing further plans or actual project developments that would modify the natural
environment of the coast. (See Appendix B, below,
for a selection of more-extensive descriptions of
state programs illustrating the several patterns
summarized in this section.)

THE LOCAL AND REGIONAL SETTING

E. Jack Schoop has described the most extensive
and most successful local and regional management
plan that now exists--the San Francisco Bay Plan.
The quality and scope of the San Francisco effort
have been so extraordinary that it serves as a natural
baseline and starting point for every Coastal Zone
management plan that is currently being launched.
This is certainly the case, for example, in North
Carolina, which is just getting well under way with
its state planning process for Coastal Zone management. As Schoop observed, the San Francisco Bay Plan
is, indeed, a workable model of a management system.

The word "system" is rather overworked lately,
but the Bay Plan is very much a Coastal Zone management system. It included background studies of
every significant potential use and value of the
Bay's resources; an interim permit mechanism over
dredging and filling, to maintain the status quo
during the planning process; a careful delineation
of major conservation and development policy recommendations; and an over-all recommended Bay Plan,
with appropriate tools of administration, including
a permanent regional agency to carry out the plan
and permanent controls over dredging, filling, and
other activities that might despoil the Bay. Although
the compromise interim political solution that
emerged from these recommendations may have fallen
short of the ideal, it is quite obvious that nothing

LEGAL AND INSTITUTIONAL CONSIDERATIONS 53

nearly so substantial would have been achieved but for the momentum behind the Bay Commission's recommendations.

Unfortunately, the San Francisco Bay Area is exceptional, if not unique, in the realm of local and regional Coastal Zone management systems. A very wide gap exists between the scope and effectiveness of the San Francisco Bay Plan, on the one hand, and the efforts of local or regional governments elsewhere, on the other hand. In most cases, literally <u>none</u> of the major elements of the San Francisco plan and management system have been accomplished on an area-wide basis. At best, an occasional municipal or county planning agency has achieved some measure of success in formulating a traditional city or county "plan" and is beginning to implement the plan through the usual land-use control measures, such as zoning, and related steps.

SOME MODELS OF ALTERNATIVE INSTITUTIONAL ARRANGEMENTS

In trying to analyze legal and institutional aspects of Coastal Zone management systems, one necessarily must address oneself to proposals and processes that tend to be vague and loosely defined. In an attempt to avoid this problem, several hypothetical situations--or models--will be posited here for discussion. Since H. Gary Knight deals with the relationship between Coastal Zone management systems and outer continental shelf management in Chapter 5, below, the remarks here will be limited to estuaries and the Coastal Zones.

A number of models can be used for this purpose; however, in order to stay within reasonable bounds, this analysis will treat only five models, chosen because they best illustrate some weaknesses as well as strengths, some problems as well as solutions, that are to be found at various levels of government and with various approaches. These five models are a local management model, a state management model, a federal management model, a multiple-jurisdiction (or eclectic) management model, and a litigation model.

A Local Management Model

In the local sphere, one might consider a local government effort by a city or a county to regulate and control or to exclude an extractive industry that proposes to locate or has located a new installation at or near the community in question--for example, some form of surface mining, such as phosphate mining or rock quarrying. Assume that a phosphate mining and processing operation, consisting of several separate companies, is located along one of the coastal sounds and that, from one or several sources at these plants, phosphates are periodically allowed to escape from the mining or processing operation. When phosphates combine with sufficient quantities of nitrogen compounds, in a body of water such as a lake or perhaps a sound, there is a real possibility of intense eutrophication and eventual pollution of the body of water. (This is the process that has severely degraded Lake Erie.)

In this instance, assume, further, that there is already a substantial amount of phosphates in the stream feeding the sound and probably also nitrogen compounds. Before long, signs start to appear in the sound that might be read as the beginning of the process of eutrophication--concentrations of algae and plant growth, and the like. Some of the local citizens in one of the counties down-sound from the mining complex get agitated and convince the Board of County Commissioners that something ought to be done. The County Commissioners are persuaded to adopt an ordinance that declares it to be a nuisance for anyone to allow or cause the introduction of substances into the sound by mining operations or otherwise that bring about or tend to bring about the condition of eutrophication of the sound and that goes on to prohibit these practices. Then, an effort is made to prosecute an alleged violator of the ordinance and what happens?

Often, there is a real problem of identifying

LEGAL AND INSTITUTIONAL CONSIDERATIONS 55

just who caused this condition. There are several separate companies in the phosphate complex, plus upstream sources of phosphates and nitrates, and the exact sources of the phosphates reaching the sound may not be clear. It is quite possible that the prosecution would falter over this matter of proving causation--and, incidentally, the same difficulty might exist if a civil action were brought instead of a criminal prosecution.

Assuming, however, that the causation problem can be solved, the next issue that is raised in this prosecution is the authority of the county to regulate this conduct at all. This issue has two facets. First, there is the question of whether the county has territorial jurisdiction to regulate this activity. If the plants are located in another county, the answer is probably no. Even if the plant is in the county, there might be some question of whether the sound itself is partly or entirely outside the county's boundaries or regulatory jurisdiction. (These are issues of the same general nature, for example, as questions of whether either a local government or a state government has authority to regulate oil-well drilling in adjacent ocean waters --or whether this is a subject only for federal regulation.)

Second, and more serious, is the question whether the statutes currently on the books empower any county to control this kind of pollution or to regulate mining concerns in this fashion. If North Carolina law was being discussed, for example, there is no statute that is plainly addressed to this matter; at best, there are some general powers to adopt ordinances to prevent and abate nuisances and to regulate or prohibit, in the interest of the public welfare, all things detrimental to the public.

These are the so-called general police powers of local governments. In interpreting local police powers such as these, the courts in most states-- certainly in North Carolina--have rather consistently read the statutes vary narrowly. This proclivity is so marked that it even has a name, Dillon's

Rule, after a legal text writer and former judge who was one of the first to express the rule in words. There is no certainty that an effort to enforce this particular local antipollution ordinance would stumble over the ghost of Judge Dillon, since the courts might consider this an abatement of a nuisance; but experience has shown that this is not likely.

Now, vary the factual situation slightly here. Assume that the prosecution of the phosphate companies does stumble over Dillon's Rule, and, at the next state legislative session, this county or some cities in the area decide to try to obtain the statutory authority that they need in order to control this pollution successfully. They have a bill drafted for introduction by their State Senator, and it covers the problem in no uncertain terms. But the State Senator advises that he does not believe that a state-wide law on the subject will ever pass, so they settle for a local bill that applies only to this one county or to several counties in the neighborhood, and it passes.

What legal problems await the enforcement of this local act, if any? Taking North Carolina as an example, the statute may be in deep trouble. Although North Carolina has a flourishing legislative tradition of local bills, its state constitution contains some restrictions on local legislation There is a provision (Article 2, Section 29) that prohibits the General Assembly from acting through local legislation--and, therefore, in effect, restricts the Assembly to general, state-wide legislation on these matters--concerning a list of a dozen or so subjects. Two of the prohibited subjects are acts regulating mining or manufacturing and acts relating to health, sanitation, and the abatement of nuisances. It is not clear beyond a doubt that a local bill on the subject described above would fall in either of these prescribed categories, but there is a likely possibility that it would. Careful drafting might help avoid the prohibition on local bills regulating mining or manufacturing, but the other prohibition is harder to circumvent.

LEGAL AND INSTITUTIONAL CONSIDERATIONS

One final issue must be raised on this subject. Assume that a statute were drafted that surmounted all the legal obstacles--that is clear enough to overcome Dillon's Rule and that is a state-wide enabling statute on regulation of environmental harzards of surface mining for all local governments, thus avoiding the issue of constitutional restrictions on local legislation. Is there a debatable policy issue concerning the appropriate distribution of power between state and local governments here, which would suggest that this is an unwise law?

At a recent meeting of a legislative study commission on surface-mining regulation, a vigorous argument was made by a mining-industry spokesman that this is not good policy, because it imposes on the industry the potential risk of having to respond to a different kind of regulation in each county of the state, which could present quite a problem, especially for a company in a business like sand and gravel mining with quarries all over the map. The issue is one of uniform state-wide controls versus discretion for localities so desiring to protect themselves with a higher level of quality than under state regulation--even, if necessary, to the extent of prohibiting certain kinds of industry or mining. Actually, it is doubtful that a law denying local discretion in such matters would hold up for very long.

The question of local competence to deal with issues of environmental pollution has not been touched upon. The answer here, of course, may vary with the size of the local community. But, at least in the case of small towns and cities or sparsely settled coastal counties, this may be a good question to ask.

A State Management Model

In order to focus on the role of state government in Coastal Zone management, one might look at a suggestion that has been voiced occasionally of late--the notion of instituting state zoning in the coastal plain region or in the entire state. The idea derives obviously from experience at the local government level, to which it is indigenous. Observing the local zoning process, one can see an obvious analogy to the need for land-use regulation in order to achieve certain objectives and goals in estuarine and Coastal Zone management. Local zoning, certainly in the coastal areas of the Carolinas, has not always been noted for its vigor, scope, or effectiveness. Finally, one might conclude that surely the state government can do it better, while achieving the goals conceived by various state governmental officials. The logic of this argument seems compelling. What, if anything, are its flaws or problems?

The principal flaw, if any, lies in the assumption that the state can necessarily do a better job of zoning than local government can, either on a regional or a state-wide basis. State government is undoubtedly best suited to handle some kinds of regulation, because of their nature or scope. Matters of state-wide concern, matters that require expertise or competence that is more likely to be available to the state government than to the local government, and matters wherein the state is more likely to be able to resist developmental pressures--all of these may fall in this category.

It is conceivable that, for one or another of these reasons, it might be advisable, at least experimentally, for the state government to be given zoning control or similar powers in some places. A special state-wide concern, combined with questions about the ability of a locality withstand developmental pressures, might point to this conclusion, for example, with respect to areas contiguous to state parks or to some portions at least of the seacoast. But it is a long step from this possibility to an argument for state zoning generally or for state zoning for the entire coastal plains or Coastal Zone region. Several interrelated factors raise questions concerning the advisability of this long step.

LEGAL AND INSTITUTIONAL CONSIDERATIONS 59

One has but to tabulate the number of members of local planning boards and zoning boards of adjustment and the hours that they devote to the zoning process to recognize that the state would be undertaking a very large order indeed, if it pre-empted the zoning field. Most of the time that these unpaid local volunteers devote to their work is unavoidable. Either it is necessary to order to meet statutory or underlying constitutional requirements of procedure or it is necessary as a practical matter in order to give satisfaction to the person whose interests are involved, or both.

Also, to shift the responsibility for zoning matters from local to state government would run counter to significant trends of the zoning movement. In the early days of zoning, city planners posited that they could establish general categories of zoning districts and zoning criteria and then leave the process alone to run itself. By contrast, today, most planners feel an increasing need for individualized and flexible attention to zoning matters by planning professionals, local governing and planning boards, and zoning boards of adjustment. Many of the most recently developed devices of zoning trade implement these notions by permitting tailor-made handling of problems that do not readily fall into the traditional zoning categories. Some examples of these devices follow:

1. "floating zones," which are pre-fabricated for use where and when needed

2. "cluster zoning," which accommodates development of tracts in compliance with over-all density requirements, but without regard to specific yard, area, or frontage requirements

3. "special permits," which designate some uses that may be permitted in special districts on approval of the planning board or the city council

4. "planned-unit development," which leaves initiative to the developer, subject to later review by zoning and planning officials.

All of these devices are responsive to a perceived need for flexibility and individualization, and all require extra time and attention from public officials and boards for their administration. The need for personalized attention for other individual matters, such as hardship cases, has long been reflected in various procedures administered by boards of adjustment. In the face of this definite trend toward more particularized treatment of zoning issues, one may well ask if it is desirable to establish a single-state system that must either require everyone to bring his zoning problems to the State Capitol or create many regional offices that may be less competent and more bureaucratic than their present local counterparts are.

Other factors reinforce these basis questions about the wisdom of a shift to state zoning. In zoning, as in other areas of public administration, many new and original ideas can be traced to experimental efforts of local planners to cope with particular local problems. One must consider whether it is worth sacrificing this source of innovation and new ideas that are generated by the present system. Finally, there are varying needs environments, and preferences from area to area within the state. It seems more sensible to handle these variations locally, rather than forcing them into a single-state pattern or into a set of regionalized patterns that will be difficult to justify to state policymakers. These, then, are some observations that come to mind in considering proposals for state zoning.

A Federal Management Model

In lieu of an analysis of a federal management model, a cross reference will be made here, by way of reminder. This is partly to save time and partly

LEGAL AND INSTITUTIONAL CONSIDERATIONS

because the job of critical analysis of a strong federal management model has already been very well done by others. The cross reference is to the Dingell bill, H.R. 25. The main features of the bill are summarized in the Secretary of the Army's agency report to the House Committee on Merchant Marine and Fisheries, on the Coastal Zone management bills as follows:

> These bills would authorize the establishment of a national system of estuarine areas in furtherance of a declared policy to preserve, protect, develop, and where possible, restore and make accessible to the public such areas for sport and commercial fishing, wildlife conservation, recreation, and scenic beauty. Areas would be designed as part of the system 1) by Congressional action on recommendations made by the Secretary of the Interior, through the President, after comprehensive studies by the Secretary or 2) by agreements between the Secretary and the States. The bills would provide advance authority for the Secretary of the Interior to acquire and administer designated areas, including authority to issue zoning regulations and to prohibit certain kinds of activities within the areas. In addition, the bills would establish permit and regulation authorities under the Secretary of the Interior which would require his approval of dredging, filling, dumping, and discharge of refuse in estuarine zones and in the Great Lakes before such activities could proceed.

In addition, the Department of the Interior permit could have been denied if the Secretary of the Interior determined that the proposed work would "reduce the quality of the affected water below applicable water quality standards, or . . . [would] unreasonably impair the natural values of any estuary." Under these broad standards, federal views and determinations would almost certainly have superseded any contrary state position.

Although there was some support for this measure, vigorous exception was taken to it in many quarters. The Army Corps of Engineers was displeased at the threat of competition with its navigable waters permits and stressed the superiority of a single permit system over a multiple permit system. The state governments were displeased at the prospect of federal regulatory action in this field, hitherto reserved to nonfederal action. Their spokesman generally stressed the virtues of evolving state estuarine-area programs and expressed objections in constitutional and political terms. Local governments did not relish the specter of federal zoning activity where before there had been only local activity and voiced objections similar to those of the state governments.

The Dingell bill had some conservationist and congressional support, but its detractors plainly outnumbered its advocates. The published hearings conducted in 1967 on this bill and its companions by the Subcommittee on Fisheries and Wildlife conservation of the House Committee on Merchant Marine and Fisheries, published under the title Estuarine Areas, are well worth reading or rereading.

A Multiple-Jurisdiction Management Model

So far, a full-fledged Coastal Zone management model has not been discussed here. At the local and state levels of government, partial systems have been examined that have dealt with only a discrete slice of the Coastal Zone management problem. The federal level has been treated only parenthetically. At this point, an attempt will be made to discuss something resembling a full-fledged management model. This will be a multiple-jurisdiction model that rides with the tide of current proposals and contemplates an over-all Coastal Zone management system, drawing on a mixture of federal, state, and

LEGAL AND INSTITUTIONAL CONSIDERATIONS

local sources. It is a typical lawyer-administrator concoction, striving to glean the best from a variety of sources--for lack of a better term, an "eclectic" management model.

This model would closely resemble what Adams has described in Chapter 2, above. It would contemplate a program of governmental regulation and land acquisition. Primary reliance would be placed on the state government, where it was willing, to regulate dredging, filling, and other alterations in estuaries. Primary reliance would be placed on local or regional governments to regulate land use throughout the Coastal Zone, subject to state regulation of estuarine alteration.

In an area that is identified in some fashion as being of paramount public concern--because what happens in the area may have significant environmental effects--the local regulation would be subject to state review. Outside that area, local regulation would be independent (subject to existing state controls over such matters as air and water pollution). At the federal level primarily, there would be a substantial system of federal financial and technical aid to the states, to assist in program development and implementation.

Coordinated with the regulatory functions would be an active long-range effort to acquire high-priority estuarine lands, at whatever level of government. The state program would be administered through a single key agency that would either perform or coordinate all important state functions in the area. The ladder principle would be followed--that is, of moving up one level of government if performance at the next lower level did not meet prescribed criteria.

There is much to be said on the plus side for this orthodox, marble-cake governmental venture. Indeed, it has already been said many times over-- not only, of course, in the context of estuarine and Coastal Zone management--and these refrains will be repeated again, often, in the future. For, after all, such an approach economizes in governmental structure by attempting to use the best of what there is and to encourage the upgrading of the remainder. It minimizes the creation of new governmental departments and agencies. It tries to make the best of local, state, and federal energies. It seeks to involve the hearts and souls of as many persons and organizations that can be involved usefully and productively in the program. It adheres to proven principles of political and administrative organization.

All of these good things and many more can be said to this approach. There are, however, certain problems involved in it, which will now be identified.

The Problem of Definition of Territory

It must be recognized that there are some perennially thorny legal problems of definition or identification. As any lawyer or administrator who has been through this mill will admit, it is more than a challenge--it is frequently a series of defeats--to try to define territorially what one is after in the estuaries and the adjoining coastal areas. In particular and concretely, what is an estuary, or a coastal wetland, or navigable waters?

In this model, the problem is compounded because it requires two sets of territorial definitions: one in aid of dredging and filling controls and the other in aid of efforts to identify where a local regulation will be paramount and where it will be subject to state review. If one turns to land acquisition to supplement or replace regulation, the legal problems of definition in the coastal region are certainly no easier, and perhaps only harder.

Basically, one can approach the definition effort either as a matter of exclusion, of delineation of land area, or of inclusion. In defining by exclusion, one would leave the task of assigning meaning mainly to judges and administrators, subject to such exclusion as is specified in the statute.

LEGAL AND INSTITUTIONAL CONSIDERATIONS 65

(Example: "for purposes of this statute, the term 'navigable waters' shall not include reservoir projects owned or operated by the United States.") In defining by delineation of land area, one might limit the statute's application to certain counties or other political subdivisions. This might serve some purposes adequately, but is unlikely to be a general-purpose solution.

Defining by inclusion is likely to be quite difficult. In some instances, a cross reference to something pre-established on a map or document may be feasible (see, for example, North Carolina General Statute, Section 113-229 [n][2]). A related approach, used, for example, in Connecticut, provides for an initial inventory of the areas involved, followed by the establishment of administrative boundaries on a map or on the ground (Connecticut Public Act No. 695 of 1969). North Carolina, in its current planning phase, is eyeing the latter approach.

This procedure seems promising, although it is no cure-all for legal difficulties. For example, one must persuade the courts and the legislature to credit the administrative determination. Also, some key term must be used; if, in making this choice, one attempts to leave something to the imagination, a constitutional hurdle of delegation of powers must be cleared. Currently, North Carolina is toying with the popular term "public trust lands" as a dividing line between local and state paramount jurisdiction.

Constitutional Questions of Due Process and Just Compensation

Another set of unavoidable legal problems in any such regulatory scheme revolves around the constitutional requirements of substantive due process or just compensation. Estuarine-protection regulations often place rather stringent limitations on the uses to which estuarine lands may be put. As a result, the enforcement of these regulations may well raise the question whether, in a particular case, the application of the regulations amounts to an uncompensated taking of property or a deprivation of property without due process, contrary to constitutional guarantees. Although landowners may validly be required to bear the external costs of their activities, government may not require owners to do something for public benefit without compensation.

Careful drafting of regulations to spell out permitted profitable uses of land adequately will, of course, enhance the chances of passing the test of constitutionality. But the courts have traditionally taken the view that every property-owner must be afforded a reasonable range of alternative uses of his property, and the courts will be very reluctant to authorize "sterilization" of land through land-use regulations. Nevertheless, some state courts have apparently sustained land-use regulations clearly found by legislative judgment to be essential and closely linked to comprehensive, evenhanded planning intended to promote the welfare of an entire region, even though the regulations result in a very substantial diminution in land value. The San Francisco Bay Plan at least proceeds on this theory in not providing for compensation to owners whose land use is restricted by dredging and filling restrictions.

To the extent that some lands in the estuarine areas may be found to be "public trust lands," there may be a means of avoiding these constitutional strictures. Plainly, no simple or all-embracing answer is available to these questions. At the very least, a careful review of the trend of decisions and public policy in each jurisdiction will be necessary as the foundation for an answer.

In the Massachusetts statute authorizing regulation of dredging and filling, there is a provision that opens a prompt and convenient access for landowners so desiring to bring the issue of compensation to the court for adjudication prior to the application of the regulations (Massachusetts General Law, Section 130-105). This offers the possibility of maintaining an effective plan and

LEGAL AND INSTITUTIONAL CONSIDERATIONS

simultaneously providing for compensation to property-owners who might otherwise successfully challenge the regulations as an unconstitutional taking of property. This safety-valve provision merits consideration by other states.

Administrative Organization and Financial Management

The stresses and strains of an eclectic management model will nowhere be more apparent than in the realm of administrative organization and financial management. Coastal Zone management inherently poses problems enough for administration. To note but a few of these problems, consider the following:

1. The need to mesh in a satisfactory fashion the divergent impulses of conservation and development, an eternal problem that varies inconsiderately in each new manifestation

2. The underfed economies and fiscal stringencies that are common at least to the coastal areas of the southeastern states

3. Natural physical conditions that often pose difficult barriers to transportation and development

4. Personal qualities often characteristic of the peoples of these coastal areas--fiercely independent, proudly insular, and strongly attached to long-established local customs and traditions.

When one adds to these inherent problems the necessity of manipulating and coordinating local, state, and federal governments in a mutual management program, the challenge to effective administration in the Coastal Zone is really quite imposing. Occasionally, a present or potential regional center of government, such as the San Francisco Bay Area, may provide a solution. For the run of cases, though, the answer emerging in the current crop of federal bills is probably the most viable one--that is, a single, lead state agency to pass upon the management plan and coordinate the entire package. As others have pointed out, this is a monumental task. Before it is over, there will be many rechanneled ambitions, reshaped goals, reorganized agencies, and bruised feelings. But it is hard to see a better way of doing the job.

A Litigation Model

In several successive editions of a set of teaching materials on natural-resources law, the author has made the following observation about the common-law, or litigation, element of water-pollution abatement:

> The episodic quality of private litigation, its inability to prevent damage, problems of proof, and localism--all these contributed to the eventual failure of this 19th Century system of pollution abatement and helped to engender the momentum for modern state laws regulating water pollution.

In the next edition of these materials, the reader will probably look in vain for this rolling sentence, because recent times have seen a vigorous renaissance of this Victorian system of pollution abatement.

The private lawsuit has suddenly become a very lively vehicle for expression of concern about environmental quality. Among the various forms that this current manifestation or participatory democracy might take are suits by individuals or conservation groups to restrain developmental activities; suits to assert public trust claims, especially in estuarine areas; stockholder-derivative actions against developmental entities; actions against public officials for failure to abate pollution effectively; involvement in local land-use regulation proceedings; and participation in administrative proceedings on such subjects as water and air pollution, regulation of estuarine alterations, and sand-dune protection.

There are, of course, limitations on this strategy of environmental control, such as the heavy burden of expense for litigation and built-in procedural and substantive obstacles in the present legal system, as well as the factors noted in the author's soon-to-be revised observation, quoted above. But anyone considering institutional arrangements for Coastal Zone management should surely take this newly reopened avenue into account.

CONCLUSION

After this examination of purported institutional alternatives, one might expect a conclusion that selects and justifies the author's preference; however, this would obviously be inappropriate here, for the models that have been presented are not comparable in nature or in scope. Rather, they were chosen in order to illustrate how each level of government has certain advantages to offer to the process of Coastal Zone management and, correspondingly, labors under certain disadvantages and constraints. Hopefully, the institutional choices that are made will approach an optimal combination of these elements.

ANALYSIS*

by H. Gary Knight

THE EFFECT OF OCS ACTIVITIES ON
ADJACENT COASTAL AREAS

Geologically, the continental-shelf slope is a continuous phenomenon beginning with the upland coastal plain and extending seaward, becoming submerged, until the edge of the continental plateau is reached and the deep ocean floor begins.[1] Political policy-makers have been unable in the past to live with this unitized concept of the shelf and have, accordingly, seen fit on various occasions to divide the marine and coastal environment into several zones of jurisdiction.** This process of allocating

---

*The research for this paper, "Discussion: The Role of the Outer Continental Shelf in Systems of Coastal Zone Management," was partially supported by the Office of Sea Grant Development, National Science Foundation.

**Currently, one can identify among these zones of jurisdiction those of inland waters, the territorial sea, special contiguous zones, the continental shelf, exclusive fishery zones, the high seas, and the deep ocean floor. Many of these zones result from vertical stratification as well as horizontal, thus producing at a given geographical location as many as three separate legal regimes as one proceeds from the surface of the ocean to the subsoil beneath it.

LEGAL AND INSTITUTIONAL CONSIDERATIONS

jurisdiction has not always taken into consideration the natural systems involved but rather has been based primarily on principles of maximizing net short-term economic gain to man.

Among the most significant of these allocations of marine resources for Coastal Zone planning is that which apportions U.S. submerged lands and their resources between the federal government and the several coastal states. The Submerged Lands Act of 1953 granted the coastal states title to, and ownership of, the lands beneath navigable waters, including the natural resources thereof, within the boundaries of the respective states.[2] These boundaries were fixed at three geographical miles from the coastline, except in the case of Great Lakes states, which received grants to the international boundary, and Texas and Florida (Gulf Coast), which received, following litigation, grants to three marine leagues pursuant to a provision therefor in the Submerged Lands Act.[3] The federal government retained jurisdiction over the resources of the continental shelf from the states' boundaries seaward.

Each coastal state subsequently applied to the newly acquired submerged lands its own legal regime for the disposition of the resources thereof. Shortly after passage of the Submerged Lands Act, the Congress enacted the Outer Continental Shelf Lands Act as the vehicle for administering its portion of the continental shelf, now referred to as the "outer continental shelf" (OCS).[4]

As the federal government and the several coastal states intensified their exploitation of the resources of the continental shelf (principally oil and gas), the unavoidable conflicts of multiple use began to arise. Many of these conflicts have been reasonably well handled so far, most notable the conflict between navigational interests and offshore oil production in the Gulf of Mexico.[5] In addition to conflicts of _use_, conflicts of _jurisdiction_ arose, principally in connection with the contention of coastal states that they be able to apply state conservation rules to oil and gas production on the OCS. Only recently, however, have such jurisdictional conflicts become critical. Previously, it seemed as if what happened on the OCS had no effect upon what happened in areas under state jurisdiction, and vice versa.

As is now well known, activities undertaken on OCS lands have profound potential for both adverse and beneficial impact on the adjacent coastal state. This may take the obvious negative form of pollution, as in the cases of Santa Barbara, California, in January-February, 1969, and the Louisiana Gulf Coast in spring, 1970. Equally important, though more subtle, is the economic impact of OCS operations on the adjacent coastal state. Persons employed in OCS enterprises may live in the adjacent coastal state and utilize that state's highways, schools, and other public services, thus creating an economic impact on the area. Conversely, the presence of a strong OCS mineral operation results in substantial economic benefit to the coastal state in increased revenues and tax bases. This latter point was made repeatedly by Louisiana public officials during the 1970 suspension of OCS lease sales off the Louisiana coast. The argument for resumption of the lease sales was often made solely on the ground that the oil industry was critical to Louisiana and that continuation of the suspension could have a substantial adverse impact on the state's economy.*

---

*For example, in response to the grand jury investigation of the spring, 1970, oil-well blowout off the Louisiana coast, Governor John J. McKeithen stated, "I would hope that the grand jury would allow me to appear before them. I would like to impress upon them the thousands of jobs that Louisiana citizens enjoy because of offshore exploration and production."

Congressman Patrick Caffery of Louisiana stated in response to Secretary of the Interior Walter J. Hickel's announcement of the probable resumption of offshore leases, "I am pleased that the secretary has moved to restore oil lease sales. This action . . . will undoubtedly bring to the economy of south Louisiana a much-needed boost."

LEGAL AND INSTITUTIONAL CONSIDERATIONS 73

To sum up, living resources, oil spills, and other phenomena occurring in the offshore area display little reverence for man's legislatively enacted and expensively litigated zones of jurisdiction.[6] It is, therefore, necessary to consider the effect of OCS operations in constructing any effective system of Coastal Zone management.

THE COASTAL ZONE AS CONTEMPLATED IN CURRENT LEGISLATION

As a result of the work of the President's Commission on Marine Science, Engineering, and Resources, several bills are now pending in the Congress to establish a system of Coastal Zone management for the nation. (See asterisked note, below.) These proposed systems have been well described elsewhere, and only the geographical area to which the management systems will be applied, if adopted, will be discussed here.

In defining the Coastal Zone, the Commission's Panel on Management and Development of the Coastal Zone stated, "For this report the coastal zone is taken as the immediate shoreline, the continental shelf, estuaries, and the Great Lakes."[7] The Commission itself, however, took a somewhat narrower view for purposes of its proposed Coastal Zone management system by defining the seaward extent of the Coastal Zone as "the territorial sea of the United States."[8] In restricting the seaward limit of the Coastal Zone to the territorial sea, the Commission was obviously reflecting the current division of jurisdiction between the coastal states and the federal government resulting from the Submerged Lands Act. This approach, of course, limits the applicability of planning and management systems to be developed by the coastal states pursuant to the proposed legislation to the territorial sea, excluding the OCS.

All of the bills now before the Congress on the topic of Coastal Zone management systems either expressly or implicitly limit the seaward extent of the Coastal Zone, over which the state Coastal Zone authority will have jurisdiction, to the territorial sea of the United States or, in some cases, to the seaward extent of the coastal state's boundary.* In none of these bills is there evidence of an intent to include the OCS as a relevant factor in developing a Coastal Zone management system.

The result is that coastal states will continue to have little or no voice in policy-making for OCS lands, even though those policies, as previously noted, may have substantial impact on coastal areas and on Coastal Zone management plans adopted by state Coastal Zone authorities. It is not possible, however, to develop a rational, comprehensive management plan for the Coastal Zone without taking into consideration OCS activities, over which the states presently have extremely limited jurisdiction.

---

*S. 3183 and H.R. 14845, the administration's identical counterpart bills, provide that the Coastal Zone extends "seaward to the outer limit of the United States territorial sea." S. 3460 and H.R. 16155, the identical counterpart bills of Senator Joseph D. Tydings of Maryland and Congressman Robert N. Giaimo of Connecticut, provide as a seaward limit for the Coastal Zone "the territorial sea or the seaward boundary [of the coastal states], whichever is the farther offshore." S. 2802 and H.R. 15099, the identical counterpart bills of Senator Warren G. Magnuson of Washington and Congressman Alton Lennon of North Carolina, also utilize the standard of "within the territorial sea or the seaward boundary, whichever is the farther offshore." H.R. 14730, Congressman Lennon's original bill, does not so expressly limit the Coastal Zone; it defines the Coastal Zone as "the lands, waters, and lands beneath the waters in close proximity to the coastline and strongly influenced by each other," thus implying a narrow band of ocean. H.R. 14731 uses a definition identical to that of H.R. 14730.

LEGAL AND INSTITUTIONAL CONSIDERATIONS

CURRENT LAW AND PROCEDURE AMELIORATING NONCONSIDERATION OF OCS MANAGEMENT POLICIES

The presently existing structure in the area of OCS management policies does afford some limited amelioration of this situation, although it falls far short of an acceptable solution. In August, 1969, in the wake of criticism over the handling of the Santa Barbara, California, Channel OCS lease sale, the Department of the Interior issued new regulations concerning selection of tracts for leasing, among which was the following:

> The Director [of the Bureau of Land Management] prior to the final selection of tracts for leasing . . . shall evaluate fully the potential effect of the leasing program on the total environment. . . . To aid him in his evaluation and determination he shall request and consider the views and recommendations of appropriate federal agencies, may hold public hearings after appropriate notice, and may consult with state agencies, organizations, industries, and individuals.9 [Emphasis added.]

Thus, although the need has been recognized, the permissive character of the new regulations provides no guarantee of state, local, or individual participation in selection of OCS leasing areas or their development.

Some recently adopted federal legislation has also made progress toward a system of mutual consultation between federal agencies and those of the states and localities. The National Environmental Policy Act of 1969 provides the following in Section 102(2):

> The Congress authorizes and directs that, to the fullest extent possible . . . all agencies of the Federal Government shall--
>
> . . . .

(C) include in every recommendation or report on proposals for legislation and other major Federal actions significantly affecting the quality of the human environment, a detailed statement by the responsible official on--

(i) the environmental impact of the proposed action,

(ii) any adverse environmental effects which cannot be avoided should the proposal be implemented,

(iii) alternatives to the proposed action,

(iv) the relationship between local short-term uses of man's environment and the maintenance and enhancement of long-term productivity, and

(v) any irreversible and irretrievable commitments of resources which would be involved in the proposed action should it be implemented.

Prior to making any detailed statement, the responsible Federal official shall consult with and obtain the comments of any Federal agency which has jurisdiction by law or special expertise with respect to any environmental impact involved. Copies of such statement and the <u>comments and views of the appropriate Federal, State, and local agencies, which are authorized to develop and enforce environmental standards, shall be made available to the President, the Council on Environmental Quality and to the public.</u>[10] [Emphasis added.]

Secretary of the Interior Walter J. Hickel recently utilized this provision by providing in the notice of intent to resume lease sales off the

LEGAL AND INSTITUTIONAL CONSIDERATIONS 77

coast of Louisiana a request for comments on the proposed resumption, specifically citing the National Environmental Policy Act of 1969 as requiring an opportunity for state and local agencies to comment on the proposal. Hickel's notice provided additionally that "Members of the general public may also submit their comments and views." This is certainly a step in the right direction, but it is not directly applicable to the Coastal Zone management problem and is deficient in not making mandatory appropriate consultations with state and local agencies (rather than simply soliciting their views) with a requirement that OCS operations not conflict or interfere with plans of Coastal Zone management adopted by the coastal state pursuant to the proposed federal legislation.

Two proposals for amending the current process have also recently been made. One of these proposed solutions would add the following language to a typical Coastal Zone management bill:

> The Coastal Zone will normally include only those areas within the boundaries of the coastal states, but the Secretary [of the Interior] may approve the inclusion of other areas under federal jurisdiction and control where he determines them to have a special functional interrelationship with lands within the boundaries of the coastal state or states affected which would justify this action in light of the purposes set forth [in the Coastal Zone management bill]. The inclusion of any such federal lands within the Coastal Zone of a state or states shall not convey or diminish any rights reserved or possessed by the federal government under the Submerged Lands Act of 1953 or the Outer Continental Shelf Lands Act of 1953.[11]

This proposal, made by Robert B. Krueger in October, 1969, at the Washington Coastal Zone Management Conference, has the virtue of flexibility but the defect of permitting the lead federal agency to determine the desirability or necessity of inclusion of OCS areas within state jurisdiction for purposes of Coastal Zone management systems. As noted above, the Director of the Bureau of Land Management already has permissive power to hold public hearings and to consult with state agencies, organizations, industries, and individuals concerning selection of tracts for leasing on the OCS. Omitted from these regulations and proposals is the power of the state Coastal Zone authority to compel the administering OCS agency to develop its plans with due consideration for the Coastal Zone management plan adopted by the state.

The second suggestion is contained in a bill (H.R. 10675) that would amend the Outer Continental Shelf Lands Act to provide the following:

> The Secretary [of the Interior] shall not enter into any mineral lease . . . under this Act . . . until (1) he shall have published notice of each proposed public hearing in connection with such proposed lease not less than twenty-one days before the date of such proposed hearing . . . and (2) he shall have held such public hearings, or have afforded the opportunity for such hearings, in such areas for the purpose of enabling all interested persons to express any objections they may have to such lease.[12]

This proposal suffers from the defect of placing the public hearing too late in the process to be effective, a point to be explained later. In addition, limiting coastal state participation to a public hearing has all the limitations inherent in the public-hearing process.[13] This process was facetiously, but not altogether inaccurately, defined by Edwin T. Haefele in October, 1969, at the Washington Coastal Zone Management Conference as "A process for allowing the electorate to let off steam after you have removed the control of public choice from their hands."[14] Accordingly, something more

LEGAL AND INSTITUTIONAL CONSIDERATIONS   79

needs to be done than simply providing an opportunity for "letting off steam."

A PROPOSAL

In order to accomplish the desired objectives of federal-state cooperation in managing and developing the resources of their respective jurisdictions, present proposals for a system of Coastal Zone management should be amended to provide the following requirements. First, the Department of the Interior or any other agency charged with responsibility for administering OCS operations should be required to give written notice to each state Coastal Zone authority reasonably proximate to any proposed activity on the OCS of the nature and timing of such activity. This would include transmitting notice of areas in which industry has evidenced an interest in securing rights, even on an informal level, so that the state might participate at the earliest possible stage.

The phrase "at the earliest possible stage" is very important because, once the oil industry has invested a substantial amount of money exploring an area in which it has evidenced an interest to the Department of the Interior, it becomes, as a practical matter, very difficult to dissuade the Department of the Interior and the industry from proceeding with their plan of disposition. At these stages of substantial vested economic interest, public hearings do very much become, in Haefele's terms, processes for "allowing the electorate to let off steam after you have removed the control of public choice from their hands." Early, open lines of communication between federal and state agencies administering submerged lands is a _sine qua non_ for an orderly system of Coastal Zone development.

Second, such federal agencies should be required to hold public hearings at the earliest possible stage on any proposed disposition of OCS resources. (All of the proposed Coastal Zone management bills provide for public hearings by the state Coastal

Zone authorities in connection with the development and implementation of master plans for the Coastal Zone.)

Third, the respective state Coastal Zone authorities should be required to supply the Department of the Interior or any other federal agency charged with responsibility for administering OCS operations with copies of all master plans and legislation affecting the Coastal Zone, including any amendments or modifications thereto, as the latter occur.

Fourth, federally administered OCS operations and Coastal Zone projects administered by state Coastal Zone authorities should be compatible with the policies and the objectives established for each other, and an administrative process for achieving such compatibility should be established. Fifth, provision should be made for judicial review of any unresolved dispute between federal agencies responsible for OCS operations and state Coastal Zone authorities in cases where achievement of mutual consent to OCS or Coastal Zone operations cannot be secured.

In making these recommendations, the author is fully aware that some state and local participation, even individual participation, exists in the present rule-making and adjudicatory procedures with respect to activities on OCS lands, but believes the critical factor is that of disposition, not regulation; i.e., determining which lands shall be leased (and when) and which shall be withdrawn from disposal (and when). Certainly, it would not be practical to give state Coastal Zone authorities veto power over disposition policies of the federal government. Situations can arise, however--for example, the Santa Barbara, California, buffer zone established by the state of California--where disposition activity on federal lands could thwart well-planned management systems on the part of coastal states.

What is suggested here is that these Coastal Zone authorities or, if none should exist, other agencies of state and local government, as well as

LEGAL AND INSTITUTIONAL CONSIDERATIONS   81

individuals, should have the right to be informed
of federal disposition activities at a very early
stage (before the oil industry or other mining
industries have too great a vested interest in
exploration costs), whereby consistency between
federal disposition and withdrawal policies, on the
one hand, and coastal state management programs, on
the other, can be ensured.

CONCLUSION

In conclusion, any system of marine-resources
management that ignores the unity of nature and
relies instead on the artificial jurisdictions
established by man is not well founded, and its
results are likely to be something less than satisfactory. Man seems to be guided by a territorial
imperative, manifested in his family, neighborhood,
city, state, and national associations. For intraman
affairs, this system is workable, if regrettably
short of perfection. But, in man-nature affairs,
man cannot successfully impose his instinctual
necessities upon nature; he must play the game by
the rules as he finds them, and the coastal and
marine environment is an interdependent ecological
system not subject to artificial segmentation. If
man does not learn to cooperate with nature rather
than attempting to subdue it, he will shortly find
nothing with which to cooperate as well as nothing
to subdue.

NOTES

1. Carl M. Franklin, The Law of the Sea: Some
Recent Developments, 53 Nav. War. Coll. Bl. Bk. Ser.
16 (1961); and Aaron L. Shalowitz, Shore and Sea
Boundaries, with Special Reference to the Interpretation and Use of Coast and Geodetic Survey Data, Vol.1
(Washington, D.C.: U.S. Government Printing Office,
1962), pp. 182-83. The legal definition of the
continental shelf given in the Convention on the
Continental Shelf (U.N. Doc. A/CONF. 13/L. 55; [1964]
15 U.S.T. 471; T.I.A.S. No. 5578) differs from the

geologic definition, as follows: "For the purpose of these articles, the term 'continental shelf' is used as referring (a) to the seabed and subsoil of the submarine areas adjacent to the coast but outside the area of the territorial sea, to a depth of 200 metres or, beyond that limit, to where the depth of the superjacent waters admits of the exploitation of the natural resources of the said areas; (b) to the seabed and subsoil of similar submarine areas adjacent to the coasts of islands."

2. P.L. 31 (83d Cong., 1st sess., May 22, 1953); 67 Stat. 29; 43 U.S.C. Secs. 1,301-1,315. See, particularly, Sec. 1,311.

3. See Ibid., Secs. 1,301 (b) and 1,312; United States v. Louisiana, 361 U.S. 1 (1960); and United States v. Florida, 363 U.S. 121 (1960).

4. P.L. 212 (83d Cong., 1st sess., August 7, 1953); 67 Stat. 462; 43 U.S.C. Sec. 1,331 et seq. For a description and analysis of the administration of OCS lands, see "Study of the Outer Continental Shelf Lands of the United States", Document No. PB 188 714 (Springfield, Va.: Clearinghouse for Federal Scientific and Technical Information, 1968).

5. On the solution to this particular conflict of use, see H. Gary Knight, "Shipping Safety Fairways: Conflict Amelioration in the Gulf of Mexico," Journal of Maritime Law and Commerce, I, 1 (1969).

6. The second report of the President's Panel on Oil Spills recommended in this regard, "The occurrences of resources offshore and the multiple uses to which offshore areas are subjected are not respecters of political boundaries. Therefore, we recommend that prompt and meaningful efforts be made to incorporate the opinions, advice and policies of state and local governments into the plans for development of the Federal offshore mineral resources." See "Offshore Mineral Resources, Challenge and Opportunity," Second Report of the President's Panel on Oil Spills (1969), p. iii.

LEGAL AND INSTITUTIONAL CONSIDERATIONS   83

7. Commission on Marine Science, Engineering, and Resources, <u>Report of the Panel on Management and Development of the Coastal Zone</u> Part III, (91st Cong., 1st sess., House Document 91-42, Part 2, 1969), p.7.

8. "Our Nation and the Sea: A Plan for National Action," <u>Report of the Commission on Marine Science, Engineering, and Resources</u> (91st Cong., 1st sess., House Document 91-42, 1969), p.51.

9. 34 Fed. Reg. 13549 (August 22, 1969), amending Part 3380, Title 43 of the Code of Federal Regulations. This regulation effects the spirit of another of the recommendations of the second report of the President's Panel on Oil Spills.

10. P.L. 91-190; 83 Stat. 852 (January 1, 1970).

11. Letter from Robert B. Krueger to Congressman Alton Lennon in U.S. Congress, House Committee on Merchant Marine and Fisheries, <u>Conference on the Organization, Utilization, and Implementation of the Coastal Zones of the United States, Including the Great Lakes</u>, hearings before the Subcommittee on Oceanography of the Committee on Merchant Marine and Fisheries, House of Representatives, 91st Cong., 1st sess., 1969, p.196.

12. H.R. 10675 (91st Cong., 1st sess.), introduced on April 29, 1969, by Congressman Richard T. Hanna of California. The bill was referred to the House Committee on Interior and Insular Affairs, from which it has not emerged as of this writing.

13. See H. Gary Knight, "Organization to Deal with Coastal Zone Problems: The Local Perspective," (paper presented to First Annual Institute of Ocean Law, sponsored by University of Miami Law Center and International Oceanographic Foundation, December 10, 1969; scheduled for publication).

14. Statement of Edwin T. Haefele, in <u>Conference on the Organization, Utilization, and Implementation of the Coastal Zones of the United States</u>, p. 77.

CHAPTER 5

ECONOMICS AND MANAGEMENT OF COASTAL ZONE RESOURCES*

by Jack L. Knetsch

A great deal of national concern has been shown over the degradation of fish, wildlife, recreation, and amenity values associated with the nation's estuaries and coastal resources. It is by all accounts reasonable that this should be. It is likely that current resource allocation and development choices are resulting in significant destruction of environmental values without commensurate gains, which results, in turn, in a substantial economic loss over what might be possible under some alternative arrangement of allocation mechanisms.

A number of studies have been completed that relate to Coastal Zone and estuary management.**

---

*The research for this paper was partially sponsored by a research grant from the Bureau of Sport Fisheries and Wildlife, U.S. Department of the Interior.

**These have included the studies by the Commission on Marine Science Engineering, and Resources; the National Council on Marine Resources and Engineering Development; the Federal Water Pollution Control

ECONOMICS AND MANAGEMENT

These have produced various recommendations, and a number of legislative proposals have been made. This paper will comment on the general problem to which these are directed and suggest another component of what the author feels would be a more effective strategy for Coastal Zone and estuary management.

ECONOMIC NATURE OF THE PROBLEM

The problems to be faced in connection with maintaining and enhancing the values of the Coastal Zone and of the estuaries are not the result of the lack of morality, nor are they really the result of the lack of planning, as is often implied. Rather, these problems stem primarily from a failure of economic incentives to guide resources to their best uses, from the point of view of everybody. In important cases in the Coastal Zone, as in so many relating to pollution and other environmental quality problems, the pricing system provides a perverse incentive structure that most directly results in the real plight of environmental degradation that now exists.[1]

It is often alleged that the basic problem of Coastal Zone and estuary degradation is that the resources are being destroyed by such things as dredging, pollution, and land-fill operations. This is not the problem, but only the immediate result. Rather, the problem is that individuals are making decisions concerning estuarine resources without being made adequately responsible and accountable for their actions, which affect the output and total value of these resources. By their actions, individuals impose important external costs on others.

Destruction or alteration of estuarine resources involves economic costs far above those that the individual himself pays. These costs are not, however, being reflected in the prices by which

---

Administration; and the Bureau of Sport Fisheries and Wildlife.

those who alter the environment are guided in making their decisions. Because of the pervasiveness of nonmarket demands, external effects, and public-good characteristics of important outputs of these resources, the costs facing land developers and polluters do not reflect the true opportunity costs of altering the use of these resources.

Prices perform an important function in a free enterprise economy; however, for them to serve as a reasonable basis for social choice, the opportunities foregone in the use of resources for any given purpose must be adequately reflected in the price figures. For example, the price of labor inputs reflect the productivity of earning power of that labor in an alternative employment. Therefore, the cost of using this productive resource in any use reflects the opportunities of production elsewhere in the economy that are thereby foregone. As long as market prices reflect these opportunity costs, they adequately serve as a guide for social judgment and lead to the maximization of the total value derived from these resources.

In the case of estuarine and other coastal resources, the conditions for using prices as correct guides for resource use do not prevail--in many cases, not even approximately. Land prices in these areas simply do not reflect the important values associated with fish, wildlife, recreation, and outdoor amenities that would be lost with alteration of these important landscapes. The prices per acre of marshlands, for example, are a vast understatement of the values that would be foregone with their destruction or serious alteration. Home-site developments that destroy or preclude the production of these environmental goods do not reflect these costs in the prices of lots, thereby making them artificially cheap. What exists, therefore, is the very fundamental problem of market signals encouraging excessive pollution and excessive degradation of coastal and natural resources.

As long as land prices seriously understate the alternative values foregone and thereby fail to guide the resolution of the conflicts inherent in competing demands, nothing can be expected but a continuation of what is undoubtedly seriously uneconomic development--a failure to obtain the largest possible economic benefit from these resources. There is every reason to expect that land developers will continue to buy land, which is now seriously and artificially underpriced, and use this scarce resource for purposes detrimental to the production of fish, wildlife, recreation, and other environmental values. As long as they are not burdened with paying the cost imposed as a result of their actions, no incentive is provided to alter either their processes, their locations, or any facet of their operation. As long as waterway shippers bear little of the costs of important opportunities foregone in alteration of the environment or of constructing waterways, they will continue to press for increased navigational development.

NONMARKET SOLUTIONS

The responses to the situation do not, on the whole, seem particularly useful. One suggestion has been that the public acquire title to these important resources. In limited cases, this may be necessary, but this fails to recognize the basic cause of the problem and is likely to be in a large sense ineffective in terms of the total problem. It may not improve on either the efficiency of recource use or the equity problems inherent in the present incidence of gains and losses. There is, further, a degree of inflexibility built into such a course of action that may well pose other problems.

The response of increased reliance on plans and planning, with the implication of a wider use of zoning and other land-use controls, similarly is unlikely to achieve altogether desirable results. One difficulty, for example, is that designating certain estuarine areas for development and others for preservation confers large windfall gains and losses on these resource owners. Experience with plans elsewhere cannot generally make one very sanguine about their effectiveness here.

The use of subsidies to pay communities and others to treat certain cases of quality degradation, although perhaps necessary in certain cases to catch up, by and large establishes patterns that reward those who do the most serious damage and, further, fails to provide incentives that encourage less costly actions.

AN ALTERNATIVE APPROACH: MARKET SIMULATION

An alternative approach for dealing with uneconomic degradation of estuarine and coastal values might consist basically of a means to make the prices that guide resource decisions in these areas reflect the true costs that are incurred by reason of resource alteration or destruction. By utilizing the pervasive influence of economic forces rather than attempting to counter them, such a scheme could be expected to lead to an over-all improvemtnt in the utilization of these resources, accomplishing it more efficiently and equitably.

The social values, which are not now reflected in prices, could be made to do so by the imposition of some form of development charge or fee. Such a payment could be levied on resource users who would alter the resource to the detriment of environmental values. If, for example, destruction of a marsh would cause a loss in fish and wildlife or other values--which are not now considered in the sale price of privately held land--a fee could be imposed on a resource-use change to make the total cost faced by the potential developer reflect the true cost of his actions.

At present, these very real, and in many cases undoubtedly large, values are now effectively taken to be zero. In no way do they enter the decision to alter or destroy the natural productivity of these resources. A far greater total output could very well be gained, with less cost, and very likely substantially less, by altering the incentive structure.

ECONOMICS AND MANAGEMENT   89

   To be efficient, of course, the charge on resource change would have to take into account explicitly the varying productivity of the environmental value of individual parcels that would be disturbed. That is, a higher charge would be levied for disturbing a more productive marsh than a less productive one. The amount of the charge would also have to vary with the actual costs that would be incurred by different forms and types of land-use changes. Developments that would destroy wildlife and environmental values would be charged a maximum, with a lesser amount levied for partial destruction. The scheme could also include the possibility of a negative payment or reward for resource-use changes that would enhance the productivity of environmental values. This variation in charge level would provide additional incentive to vary the nature of the resource change in the direction of preserving more natural values.

   A charge schedule must necessarily establish differential levies to provide the desired incentives and restraints. This, in turn, necessitates a classification of estuarine and coastal areas that would reflect, to the best of current knowledge, the relative productivity of these different land resources. Although this is a major test of information, the value question looms as large, although perhaps not as explicit, in the design of the plans called for in many alternative management proposals. That is, the weighing of values is here in either case.

   The fees would reflect the environmental values--including fish, wildlife, recreation, and scientific, scenic, and other similar values--that would be involved in the resource-use change and that are not now reflected in the prices. In this way, those parcels of land that are in greatest demand for, say, home-site development would be developed for that purpose much more in areas where the environmental values were smaller in comparison to the development values; that is, where it is less costly. This, of course, is desired if, in fact, all of the costs are appropriately considered.

   Change would come about differentially, with

competing demands for resources being reflected by the new "prices." Choices would then be made so that, by and large, the more productive estuarine and coastal areas would not be developed, for they could, in effect, bid resources from other uses. Developers would find those parcels with a lower environmental value comparatively less costly, and, consequently, development would proceed on these lands to a greater extent relative to the others. Further, as development proceeded, the remaining undeveloped areas could have still higher fees imposed to reflect an increasing scarcity value. In effect, the charge being proposed is a price to a land developer, or to anyone who would alter the estuarine environment, for the total cost of the resources used.[2]

Another possibility, which should not be ignored, is to levy a charge on the beneficiaries of preserving the current resource use. If preservation of saltwater marshes maintains the productivity of a fishery, then those who benefit from this could be asked to pay the costs of opportunities that are foregone. In principle, economic efficiency of the results differs little, but the consequences of the distribution of the gains and losses vary greatly. The point is the one raised in connection with water-pollution abatement. It matters little, in terms of ultimate resource-use efficiency, whether the polluter pays a charge for the costs incurred to others as a result of his polluting or if the downstream water users pay him a bribe not to pollute. There are, of course, reasons to favor the first alternative in pollution cases and probably likewise in the case of estuarine and coastal resources, but more examination is needed.

RESEARCH NEEDS

This proposal would impose severe strains on current knowledge of the relative productivity of coastal resources. Although there is insufficient information for an optimum solution, the knowledge is sufficient to implement a scheme to make greatly improved allocations. Some judgments must be made in any event, but making the value questions more explicit would aid in utilizing current information in a meaningful way. It would also provide a focus and incentive for research efforts to improve these value determinations.

There is a parallel here with the relative ignorance on assessing the losses and benefits of water-resources developments at the time of the passage of the 1936 Flood Control Act, which established the necessity for an explicit benefit-cost analysis of each project. Since this incentive was provided, a great deal of good research has now yielded very tolerable estimates of a variety of gains and losses associated with water development. Very much the same thing could be expected in the current case.

As more precise information becomes available on relative values, the charge schedules could be adjusted to take this into account. Furthermore, after initial charges are established the patterns of resource changes could be observed; and, as certain types of areas become relatively more scarce, this too could prompt changes in the charge schedules.

INSTITUTIONAL ARRANGEMENTS

The charge levels would have to be set by federal agencies. This would be necessary to counter the economic motives for individual states to set their charges so as to maximize economic values that accrue to them that may, in fact, not be in the best interest of the nation as a whole. Individual groups exert pressure for specific solutions that often do not represent the best interest for all, and a higher jurisdictional unit would be more appropriate to make a decision from the standpoint of the gains and losses involved.[3] The splintering and fragmentation of authority is often cited as being partially responsible for many of the problems in the Coastal Zone. It would seem that this need for better coordination would be further reason for looking to the price system.

A further advantage of the suggested scheme is that it would generate revenues rather than impose on already restricted budgets. The funds that would be collected could be used for various purposes, although earmarking has its disadvantages. Some could be used for purchase of a few parcels that might, for example, be judged critical to estuarine ecology. Another purpose would likely be served by using the funds for payments to local governmental units that would be differentially adversely affected by the change in development activity brought about by this scheme.

Another advantage of the scheme is that, to the extent that purchase is necessary, the imposition of the charge system would effectively reduce the price that public bodies would have to pay for the lands acquired. The fee, by raising the price paid by developers, would bring about shifts in the demand and supply schedules to an extent that the net prices, exclusive of the fee, paid by the public bodies would be less than they would be without such an imposition of charges.

PUBLIC SUBSIDIES AND ENVIRONMENTAL DEGRADATION

Although the values of preserving resources need investigation, a parallel series of questions can be raised in connection with the need to assess the real competition offered by alternative land uses. More attention must be paid to those alternative uses whose competitive advantage is in part due to some public subsidy or similar action. Cases of this that do or have existed include, for example, the subsidies paid to maritime interests, the subsidies on waterway activities, the tax incentives offered on oil and other extractive operations, guaranteed prices for stockpiled materials, import tariffs and quotas, grants and loans for various commercial development activities, and partial public absorbtion of insurance risks for high-risk activities and locations.[4] To the extent that a public subsidy is involved in such cases, it increases the competitive

ECONOMICS AND MANAGEMENT   93

position for these activities to bid away resources
from environmental uses.

                          SUMMARY

    This proposal could usefully be considered as a
major part of a management strategy for dealing with
estuarine and coastal resource problems. Such a
strategy might include a combination of forbidding
certain uses, restricting other environmentally
destructive activities, and purchasing still others,
but the majority of cases could involve a heavy
reliance on this form of economic incentive as a
means of dealing with the problem. It builds on the
inherent nature of the cause of the current concern
and provides the incentive for more efficient and
equitable allocation of these important resources.

                           NOTES

    1. See, for example, Henry Jarrett, ed.,
Environmental Quality in a Growing Economy (Baltimore,
Md.: The Johns Hopkins Press, 1966).

    2. The parallel to the effluent charge proposal
for water-pollution control is close. See Allen V.
Kneese and Blair T. Bower, Managing Water Quality:
Economics, Technology, Institutions (Baltimore, Md.:
The Johns Hopkins Press, 1968).

    3. James A. Crutchfield, "Socioeconomic,
Institutional and Legal Considerations in the Manage-
ment of Puget Sound" (report to the Federal Water
Pollution Control Administration, August, 1969).

    4. Miller B. Spangler, "A Preliminary Review
of Alternative Federal Measures of Encouraging Private
Investment Enterprise in Marine Resource Development,"
(Washington, D.C.: National Planning Association,
May, 1968), report to the National Council on Marine
Resources and Engineering Development and the National

Science Foundation; and Ian Burton, Robert Kates, and Rodman Snead, <u>The Human Ecology of Coastal Flood Hazard in Megalopolis</u> (Chicago: University of Chicago, Department of Geography Research Papers, 1969).

ANALYSIS

by William A. Ward

First, the author should like to applaud Professor Knetsch for his valiant and informed attempt to bring economic logic to bear upon the problems of estuarine management. Second, since the author has been asked as an economist to critique the above presentation, he shall attempt to be critical of the proposed approach--perhaps pedantically critical in places. Finally, having discharged his responsibility as a discussant, he will do what is generally done by discussants--present his own viewpoints on the matter, however unrelated to the principal paper.

Knetsch advocates a system of charges to those who would convert estuaries to commercial and residential uses. He argues that this approach would lead to a more efficient and equitable utilization of the estuarine resource. From an economist's viewpoint, however, his approach is neither necessarily more equitable nor more efficient. Although the author's arguments regarding the two are somewhat intertwined, they basically revolve around two issues: the implicit problem of defining the relevant property rights and the realization that the market imperfections that brought about the problem will not have been corrected by his approach.

THE QUESTIONS OF PROPERTY RIGHTS

The basic problem in the case of the estuaries

is the definition of the property rights of the productive capacity of the marshlands. The problem is essentially the same in all pollution issues. Knetsch states two alternative approaches to solving the problem: charging a conversion tax to land developers or having the fishermen and other environmental resource users pay for having the estuaries remain in their current use. These alternatives would, in effect, give a choice as to who should own the productive capacity of the resource. (Currently, several such property-rights issues are developing, as concern over pollution mounts; property rights to air, water, and views are examples).

There is, apparently, some current dispute over who should own the rights to the environmental-goods capacity of the estuaries--the public at large or the landowner. Consumers of the environmental goods produced by the estuaries are, in effect, claiming a right to the continued production of those goods. The dispute comes in the confrontation of these claimed rights with the long-accepted American tradition regarding rights of landed property-owners. The real issue boils down to whether landowners are going to continue to be given dictatorial rights over the governance of these resources, regardless of the side effects upon other property.

In such questions concerning property rights, "equity" is a very difficult concept to handle. The economist is not particularly well equipped to handle the problem of property conferral and neither are most other people, including the well-schooled philosopher.[1] Fortunately, both Knetsch and the author belong to a social science discipline that has a very well-developed body of practicable theory. This theory can handle the efficiency and welfare implications of all sorts of economic changes. Unfortunately, however, one of the changes that economists can not handle very well is that of institutional change, and the institution of property rights is one of the most basic of these institutions.[2] Thus, on the basis of economic theory, it is not really possible to determine whether a given property-right alteration would leave society any better off.

Under a reasonably rigorous definition of efficiency, it is doubtful that economists could say whether a given institutional change were more <u>efficient</u>, either.[3]

WHO BEARS THE COST?

The discussion here of the second issue is based upon Knetsch's attempt to force the <u>land developer</u> to pay the full opportunity cost of the development of coastal marshlands. First, the opportunity cost would be borne not by a land developer purchasing the land for development, nor by ensuing purchasers; the cost would be borne by the owner at the time of the property-rights redefinition. As Knetsch knows, the charge would not raise the <u>value</u> of <u>all</u> such units for land development; it would merely reduce the volume of such conversion and raise the scarcity price of those parcels converted. Most of the price increase would be taxed away. (The principle is similar to the appreciation in capitalized land values realized by tobacco farmers when the production control program was initiated. The initial owner realized all of the gain in future income streams through its capitalization into the price of his tobacco land.) If the developer is anyone besides the initial owner, the tax will not be borne by the real culprit. Thus, there is some question as to the equitability of the incidence of the tax.

Second, the approach to charging converters of estuarine resources does not correct the market and pricing imperfections involved. The charge for land development is perhaps capable of reflecting the real opportunity cost of the environmental goods; however, raising the cost on one side will not substitute for the exchange process. The process of barter and exchange allows both parties to a transaction to increase their real welfare by trading. Thus, if the fisherman <u>could</u> buy out the developer, both would be made better off. In the Knetsch proposal, however, the effective trade will not be between the relevant environmental-goods consumers and the land developer; it will be between the land developer and the government. Insofar as the taxing unit and the consumers are not identical sets--that is, composed of exactly the same individuals--the market is still not approximated.

For instance, consider the situation of an industrial polluter, say in Detroit. The firm disposes of its solid wastes into the Detroit River and into the air over Detroit. Both of these methods are destructive of the environmental values of Detroit residents. (Perhaps they have a long-run effect on the rest of the world, but the brunt is borne by Detroit residents.) The federal government can impose a charge upon the firm, similar to Knetsch's land development charge. The firm can choose to pay the charge and continue dumping at the old level. Supposedly, then, compensation has been made. The compensation, however, goes to the federal treasury, not to the down-wind or down-river resident. If the revenues are then distributed on a population basis, Detroit gets about 5 per cent of it. The down-wind residents might well get none of that.

The initial problem was that there was no market for environmental goods. This was because the air could not be captured and sold and because the residents could not organize to buy the rights to clean air because of the exclusion problem. The charge will not have substituted for such a market, however, because of the difference in the parties to the transaction. The segments paying the costs and receiving the benefits are different. The problem here is similar to the problem in the federal water-resources program. There, the cost of public works is borne basically by the federal treasury. Thus, the nation as a whole pays the cost.

For most projects, however, the benefits are very localized to project areas. Thus, the local area can receive all of the benefits of a project while only paying a small proportion of the costs. Each area pushes to maximize its share of the budget. All of them working together, then, push up the entire budget. The relative welfare of a part and

ECONOMICS AND MANAGEMENT   99

the over-all welfare of the whole are in conflict.
Each part acting alone leads to a nonoptimum over-all
allocation.[4] Thus, one should be very careful that
the remedy designed does not simply substitute another
problem. In the case of market failure and intervention, the program must simulate the desired market
if the desired result is to be achieved.

GEOGRAPHIC DISTRIBUTION OF INCOME

Knetsch does not discuss the issue of income
distribution fully enough in his treatment. Inter-
personal income distribution will be directly affected
by the way in which property rights in the estuaries
are defined. Interregional distribution could arise
as a major issue if the most environmentally productive
estuarine areas were located in one region. In this
case, the region's estuaries would, in effect, be
forced to remain in a use that produced environmental
goods (income) for the entire nation. Since the
region could not charge for these goods, the regional
income-producing value of their estuaries would be
lower than were those of other areas. Thus, although
over-all national income might be increased, the
costs would be borne by one region.

Moreover, the difference in incomes would be
greater than that reflected directly in the differential values of the estuarine lands; the industry and
commerce that would be economically linked to those
that would destroy the environmental values would
not be located in the region, either. For example,
the ubiquitous real estate agents who dot the landscape of Myrtle Beach would not find such profitable
employment in the absence of commercial development.
Thus, it is possible that relatively small differences
in charge rates between areas can have relatively
large effects upon the areas' incomes. Although
this is perhaps unimpressive to those from other
regions, the Southeasterner knows regional income
problems firsthand. He knows that the traditional
approach of maximizing efficiency and national income
now, while proposing to handle the distribution
problem later, does not work.

Measures that increase national income by increasing the difference between individuals or groups become a part of public policy. Those who profit by those measures are not about to allow them to be revised. Those who bear the cost are financially and politically powerless to do anything to rectify the problem. Thus, income disparaties get built into the system. The disparaties grow as national income grows. Dissatisfaction with the system grows as the disparaties grow.

Economists must learn to face up to the problem of the income-distribution affects of economic policies. Seldom does public intervention have only efficiency effects. Indeed, public intervention is generally necessitated because certain exchanges cannot be made at the mutual benefit of the transactors. If they could, then the market would handle the exchange, and public intervention would not be needed. Thus, to be relevant, the political economist must, in most situations, be willing and able to talk about the gains and losses, as well as to whom they accrue.

CHANGING CONCEPTS OF PRIVATE PROPERTY

Now, a very relevant institutional consideration in dealing with the problems of the estuaries must be discussed. In fact, it is important not only for the problems of the estuaries but also for many other pollution problems. It is also an issue that society must soon deal with if it is to solve many other social problems confronting it. That basic institutional consideration is the concept of rights in property. The issue of property must be dealt with as wants and scarcities change; and, in these days of rapid change, it must be dealt with more expeditiously than in the past.

One thing that should be understood first about property is that no specific form of it is either natural or immutable. Its ownership--in whatever form it may be manifest--is enjoyed only at the consent and the mutual trust of the rest of society.[5]

The mutual beneficiality of property rights is the only thing that sustains them in a society. If everyone agrees that property, as defined, benefits all, then people consent to each others' rights in property. When people no longer feel benefited by those definitions, their form will be changed and, perhaps, property will be taken away from some people.

When the prevailing form of property becomes destructive of other social values, then mutual beneficiality is lessened. When most parties no longer enjoy mutual benefit, that form should and will be changed to a more mutually beneficial form. Most people would agree that such change should occur through reasoned and logical alternatives, such as that proposed by Knetsch. Most would choose such an approach over that of revolution. To those unwilling to accept any institutional change at all, however, even Knetsch's proposal would appear revolutionary.

The task before society in handling the pollution issue (and many other social issues) is the constructive redefinition of rights in property. Unlike most of the rest of the world, the United States has given landowners the rights to all of the assets underlying their land (the air-pollution problem has raised the issue of overlying resources as well). Americans have tended to view rights in landed property as the right of the owner to use his property in any way he pleases. This extends, in some instances, to the secondary right to protect that right in any way he can (even to valuing property rights over human life--witness the recent passage of what someone has called the "Nebraska daisy-picking law," whereby a landowner can shoot a trespasser without being liable of a murder charge).

As clean air, water, views, and fish become more scarce, others are beginning to question such rights of the landed property-owner. Such declarations as "I have a right to breathe clean air" and "I have a right to an unobstructed view" are beginning to be heard. On a strictly legally defined basis, there are perhaps no such rights; but, in terms of the mutual-beneficiality definition of property, there are indeed the rights that exist in numbers. The essence of democratic rule is that, when the numbers favoring institutional change are sufficient, change can occur logically and peacefully.

The number of people who no longer enjoy the mutual benefit of current property-right definitions for estuarine resources is apparently growing. Knetsch's proposal for a charge on land conversion indicates that he is one of those not favoring the current definition. His proposal indicates that he feels that others have rights to other estuarine-related property, such as fish and other environmental goods. The precision of the techniques he possesses as an economist to evaluate the necessary readjustments under new property definitions have been questioned here, but that does not mean that the author, as a consumer of environmental goods (and as a student of the problem of their provision), does not agree with him about the need to establish a right in those goods for all of society. There is wholehearted agreement that everyone should have a property right in the products of the estuaries and in air and water.

The basic point is that society has a tremendous job in front of it in defining exactly what those rights should consist of and in determining how their effectuation is to be managed in a socially optimal fashion. Thus, although one might argue that no economist can precisely and objectively tell the welfare effects of the Knetsch proposal, one cannot argue that the proposal is not a step in the right direction. It is a big step toward forcing society to consider explicitly exactly what are the rights people confer upon one another. It is a big step toward the design of a society that functions for the mutual benefit of its members and that attempts to maximize that benefit.

NOTES

1. See Karl Mannheim, *Ideology and Utopia* (New York: Harcourt, Brace & World, 1936); also Karl Duncker, "Ethical Relativity? (An Enquiry into the Psychology of Ethics)," *Mind*, XLVIII, 189 (January, 1939), 39-44.

2. See John R. Commons, *Legal Foundations of Capitalism* (Madison: University of Wisconsin Press, 1959), chap. ii.

3. See I. M. D. Little, *A Critique of Welfare Economics* (London: Oxford University Press, 1965), chaps. viii-ix.

4. Allan Schmid and William Ward, *A Test of Federal Water Project Evaluation Procedures with Emphasis on Regional Income and Environmental Quality*, AER 158 (East Lansing: Michigan State University, Department of Agricultural Economics, April, 1970).

5. See J. F. A. Taylor, *The Masks of Society*, Des Moines: Meredith, 1966), chap. v.

CHAPTER

6

**A POLICY
ANALYSIS APPROACH:
OBJECTIVES
ALTERNATIVE DEVELOPMENT STRATEGIES
AND ECONOMETRIC MODELS***

by Maynard M. Hufschmidt,
Hugh Knox, and Francis H. Parker

This paper does not present the results of any research on South Atlantic Coastal Zone problems or issues, nor do the authors claim any intimate familiarity with the physical, economic, and social situation of the Coastal Zone. It is, rather, a means for advancing a proposed approach to research on the planning and decision-making process for the seashore and estuarine zones of North Carolina.* Some important relationships between the methodology proposed here and the issues of dynamic decision-making, flexibility, and needs for data will be discussed, however.

The material is presented in four parts:

1. A statement of the hypothesis underlying the proposed approach; namely, that modern policy analysis, involving the essential elements of systems

---

*A beginning on this research has been funded by the National Science Foundation and the state of North Carolina as a part of the marine-science research program.

analysis, is required for effective public decision-making in complex settings--economic, social, physical, and institutional--as in the Coastal Zone (including the development of a set of objectives to guide public decision-making and a systematic search for alternative means and measures for best meeting the specified set of objectives)

2. A statement of the research methodology as it relates to the initial formulation of public policy objectives, the preparation of a set of alternative development and management strategies for the Coastal Zone, and the reformulation of public policy objectives into a form useful in planning and decision-making

3. A statement of the research methodology as it relates to use of econometric models in the planning and decision-making process

4. A summary statement relating the proposed approach and methodology to planning for Coastal Zones in general and to questions of dynamic planning, flexibility, and needs for data.

THE ROLE OF POLICY ANALYSIS

The coastal and estuarine zones of the Southeastern states are now on the threshold of major change, and a desire to handle the changes wisely and creatively has been manifested. There is a determination to manage coastal resources effectively, to plan carefully and deliberately for their use, and to prevent needless despoilation of resources through tolerance of haphazard growth and development. Resource management has long been a central concept in regional planning, dating back at least seventy years to the conservation movement--to Gifford Pinchot and Theodore Roosevelt. The concept of systematic management itself is not new. It has, however, been given a boost in recent years through the emergence of systems analysis, operations research, planning-programing-budgeting systems (PPBS), and other management techniques developed initially in defense, space, and water-resource investment fields. These appear to offer new and more powerful tools for analyzing and planning large-scale systems, such as regional resource systems.

These techniques are being advanced as tools to be used in dealing with problems of the Coastal Zones. It may be useful to raise a caution concerning their use, learned through experience in regional planning and analysis. The caution deals with the type of problem for which these new management techniques are or are not applicable. The great selling point of the systems approach is that it "put a man on the moon." If systems analysis can handle the complexity of a moon shot, goes the argument, then it surely can handle the less technically complex problems of cities and regions. Systems analysts are actively seeking to apply their skills in these new areas of social concern.

Caution is also necessary lest the analogy to the complex moon shot mislead people. It is in part a false analogy. Although the process itself is incredibly complex, with far-flung scientists and subcontractors having to dovetail their work precisely, in one important respect there is no complexity at all. All of the complex activities are contributing to one very simple and straightforward goal: to put a man on the moon and bring him back safely. Everyone understands this goal. All the decisions to be made can be evaluated in light of how they affect this goal.

In the moon-shot case, very complicated systems contribute to an essentially simple and well-defined goal. This fact should be a warning about the easy transferability of systems analysis to the area being considered. In the coastal zone, individual

A POLICY ANALYSIS APPROACH   107

policy tools and techniques are being dealt with that are much less complex and esoteric than those required to propel and navigate a space-ship. The big difference is that the goals are not nearly so well defined as those of the moon shot. There is no general agreement on a single goal for which all our resources are to be managed. In the absence of such agreement, there are severe limits on the applicability of even the most esoteric systems approaches.

Management of coastal zone resources is enormously complicated by this fact. Rather than a single objective to which all parties interested in the coastal zone can subscribe, there is apt to be a set of separate objectives, around each of which different clusters of actors can rally, but all of which cannot be simultaneously maximized. For example, the traditional goal of economic development and growth implies one attitude toward resource management. This attitude is probably held by large numbers of residents in the area, by industries, by chambers of commerce, and by landowners. This goal has also been establizhed as a matter of national policy through the goals statement of the Coastal Plains Regional Commission: "To close the income gap with the rest of the nation." This goal is obviously in conflict with the goals held by many of those interested in perservation and protection of coastal resources. Management of resources may mean something completely different to those interested in developing the resources from what it means to those interested in preserving them. In the abstract, each side can make a plausible case for the validity of its position. It is only when one tries to combine the conflicting goals in an operational statement of public policy objectives that the problem becomes difficult. Everyone will agree that more jobs are needed for those living below the poverty within the Coastal Zone. They will also agree on the desirability of preserving the ecosystem of the estuaries or protecting the area's water table against salt-water intrusion. The crisis arises when they have to choose whether to accept an industry that offers jobs but harms the estuary or the water table. How much damage to the natural system is acceptable in return for providing employment and dignity for 100 poor families? Some ecologists would say none, while some economists and others concerned with social welfare might accept quite a bit.

There is no simple answer to this problem. Choices will have to be made; one desirable goal will have to be traded off against other, incompatible goals. As economic and social pressure increases in the Coastal Zone, decisions of this sort must be made with increasing frequency. Before any scientific approach to resource management can be successful, much more effort must go into the establishment of a workable and acceptable statement of goals for the Coastal Zone, or what the economist and systems analysts term an "objective function."

This will be a very difficult task, in some ways the most difficult of the entire management process. It should not, however, be avoided because it is difficult. The alternative to developing such a goal statement would be to continue as at present, permitting conflicts to arise and be settled in the white heat and emotionalism of individual situations.

This leads to a statement of the hypothesis underlying this research: that, in applying the essential elements of systems analysis to problems of the Coastal Zone, primary attention should be given to the formulation of a set of public policy objectives that are derived from the preferences of the people in the region, the state, and the nation. The emphasis is placed on deriving operational goals --in formal terms, an objective function or alternative objective funtions--to which techniques of systems analysis--econometric models, physical models, simulation, and mathematical programing methods--can then be applied.

This approach, that of combining systems-analysis techniques with explicit formulation of statements of objectives, is called policy analysis. Policy analysis deals with the major actors in the goal-setting and decision process. These are federal, state, and local governments, including the individual agencies at each level of government; private interests and interest groups; community, regional, and state leaders; and the general public. Policy analysis is concerned with the way in which goals are set and revised, alternative proposals are advanced and modified, and policy instruments--taxes, subsidies, regulations, public investments, and administrative actions--are used in the management process. This does not mean that system analytical <u>techniques</u> are considered unimportant. In fact, the research proposed on econometric models for the Coastal Zone is seen as part of a planning and decision-making approach using policy analysis.

OBJECTIVES AND ALTERNATIVE DEVELOPMENTAL STRATEGIES

At the outset, it must be recognized that an approach involving the explicit setting of objectives has major difficulties. A number of writers on planning and decision theory hold that a planning strategy that attempts to derive explicit objectives as a first step in the process is doomed to failure.[1] This is held to be especially true where there are multiple interests and jurisdictions involved, which is, of course, the case in the Coastal Zone. The approach proposed here does not disregard these valid criticisms of the underlying theory; rather, it seeks to take these factors into account in the way it builds its research methodology.

The proposed methodology consists of four major steps:

1. A review will be made of prior experience by state and local planning agencies in developing and using goals statements for states, regions, and communities. This review would reveal the pitfalls of previous attempts to use goal statements in planning and should suggest profitable means of proceeding with the analyses.

2. Preliminary sets of planning and development objectives will be prepared from existing sources. These sources include national and state legislation; statements of public policy, current plans, and programs of federal, state, and local agencies; policy positions expressed by interest groups both within and outside the region, including private enterprises, economic development groups, and conservation groups; and views of newspapers and leading public figures. This material, plus statements from the general public, will be used to develop alternative statements of objectives.

3. From these statements of objectives it is proposed to prepare, in broad terms, alternative strategies or patterns of development that would be consistent with different mixes of economic development and environmental quality objectives. These strategies will be developed in close cooperation with work now under way by the Coastal Plains Regional Commission and its contractors and by obtaining information from the many federal, state, local, and private planning and development agencies now active in the region. The econometric models discussed in the next section will be used to provide information on the relationship between sets of objectives and alternative development strategies. The purpose of this step is to show how alternative plans and programs can be formulated in a multiple-objective context.

4. These strategies or patterns of development will be submitted for reactions from planning and decision-making agencies and individuals both within and outside the region. From these

reactions it may be possible to revise
and refine the statements of objectives
so that they may be of direct use in
applying systems models to development
of "best" or "satisfactory" management
programs for the Coastal Zone.

This "feedback" method of formulating objectives and developing management programs can have more than one cycle. Basic to the approach is the emphasis on objectives and on ways of formulating statements of objectives in operational terms.

With respect to the first step--review of prior experience in developing goals statements--there is a modest amount of literature available that reports experiences largely since 1960.[2] Major landmarks are (a) the report of former President Dwight D. Eisenhower's Commission on National Goals;[3] (b) studies by the Regional Plan Association of goals for the New York metropolitan region;[4] and (c) development of a statement of goals for Dallas, Texas, patterned on the Goals for Americans approach.[5]

The state of North Carolina has been investigating the problem of goal-setting at the state level for about two years, and its Governor has recently established a state-wide committee to develop a goals statement. With specific reference to Coastal Zones, the experience of the San Francisco Bay Conservation and Development Commission in setting goals and developing policies therefrom, as reported by Schoop in Chapter 1, above, is obviously relevant; so, also, are the goals implied in the proposed federal legislation on Coastal Zone management, as reported by Adams in Chapter 2, above. In summary, it appears that there is sufficient experience and literature on goal-setting at the national, state, and local levels to give one a good start on such work.

With respect to the second step, the initial emphasis will be on a set of objectives that include at least the following: national economic efficiency, regional growth and regional income redistribution, individual opportunity and personal income redistribution, public health and safety, and protection and enhancement of environmental quality. From these rather basic objectives, specific, operational objectives will hopefully be developed, relating to level and distribution of per capita income, levels of pollution, and other measures of environmental quality, either for the entire Coastal Zone or for subregions within the zone. The many and diverse statements and positions on objectives that will be obtained from public and private groups will then be fitted into an over-all objectives framework, which may take the form of a matrix, with columns of fundamental objectives and rows of specific targets and specific public and private groups affected.

In the third step, alternative strategies or patterns of development or management that will be consistent with different objective sets will be prepared. At this time, three or four strategies are visualized, covering the spectrum from a strategy that places primary emphasis on preservation and restoration of the coastal and estuarine environment in an ecological sense, relegating economic development to a secondary role, all the way to a strategy that emphasizes economic and social development of the zone, including maintenance and even increases in population, with environmental preservation allowed only to the extent that it does not impede attainment of the primary goal.

Intermediate strategies would be developed that allow for both economic and social development and environmental preservation. Some strategies may concentrate on major development of some portions of the zone and preservation of other portions. These strategies will also be concerned with relative emphasis on public health (through drainage or use of pesticides for mosquito control), as compared to environmental preservation (through prohibition of land drainage or some types of pesticides).

The formulation of development and management strategies would serve to place in perspective specific policy issues, such as development or preservation of Smith (Baldhead) Island. Promotion or rigorous regulation of phosphate mining, encouragement or restriction of agricultural drainage of swamplands, dredging of navigation channels, and the intensive or extensive recreational use of seashores would be other policy issues involved in these strategies.

In the fourth step, as reactions are sought to the suggested strategies of development and management, information and insight will hopefully be gained on the feasibility of obtaining widespread agreement on a set of operational goals. Perhaps this is not possible; perhaps developmental activists and environmental preservationists cannot agree, and there is no substitute for a bitter and divisive fight on every specific project proposal. Hopefully, this will not be the case; this research seeks to determine the answer.

ECONOMETRIC MODELS

In using econometric models for analysis of the Coastal Zone, it is important to realize that the region is underdeveloped in many respects, with regard to the three-state region that includes it, as well as with regard to larger regional groupings, such as the Southeast, and to the entire eastern seaboard of the United States. It is underdeveloped in terms of income, human resources, social infrastructure, and, especially, its relatively unspoiled environment.

In order to plan for this region it is necessary to know the relationships among production, income, human resources, and the environment both within the Coastal Zone and between the Coastal Zone and the rest of the region, however defined, with which it has meaningful ties. The ties may be economic, involving exports and imports; social and racial, expressed through flows of migration; or environmental, relating to airsheds, watersheds, estuaries, and seashores.

At the present time, a group at the University of North Carolina is constructing an econometric model of the three-state region that includes the Coastal Zone. When the initial version is complete, hopefully by July 1, 1971, the connections between income and employment in the three-state region and at the national level will have been specified and estimated. The connections will include those relating to migration, both within the area and between the area and the remainder of the United States.

How will this relate to the problem as described above? There should be by then a better method than is currently available of projecting the impact of national changes on local policy variables, such as tax rates on regional economic activity. These changes will then be translated into demand changes for local industry, and the derived demand changes will be used for inputs to these industries. In addition to the econometric model, an input-output table for the region will be used. A South Carolina input-output table already exists, based on 1958 data, and the Research Triangle Institute is constructing one for North Carolina based on 1963 data. Of particular interest will be those sectors that have environmental dimensions; for example, mining, tourism, forestry, and fisheries. Further, there will be some indication about how public policy decisions with regard to public investment in both the social and the economic infrastructure and human resources will affect these flows.

The detail and policy usefulness of the model as it is currently being developed are far from satisfactory. Demands for data, particularly on private and public investment, cannot be met with as much precision as one would like. Further effort and resources are needed to obtain investment data; personal income data that avoid the bias of commutation patterns; and more detail on the personal characteristics, geographic origins, and destinations of migration flows.

The next question is what would be done if correct and detailed information on all the impacts

A POLICY ANALYSIS APPROACH   115

of economic development was available. There would
still be only a positive model describing what would
happen in the three-state area or in the Coastal Zone
if certain national changes occurred or if certain
local policies were adopted. Without knowing the
preferences of those with interests in the region,
one is left with a set of projections that may or
may not be useful in policy formulation. The authors
hope to do better than this.

Their hope is that the model can be framed in
the context of quantitative economic policy models
rather than in the more traditional mode of positive
econometric models. The figure below illustrates
the difference and additional complications.

Policy instruments

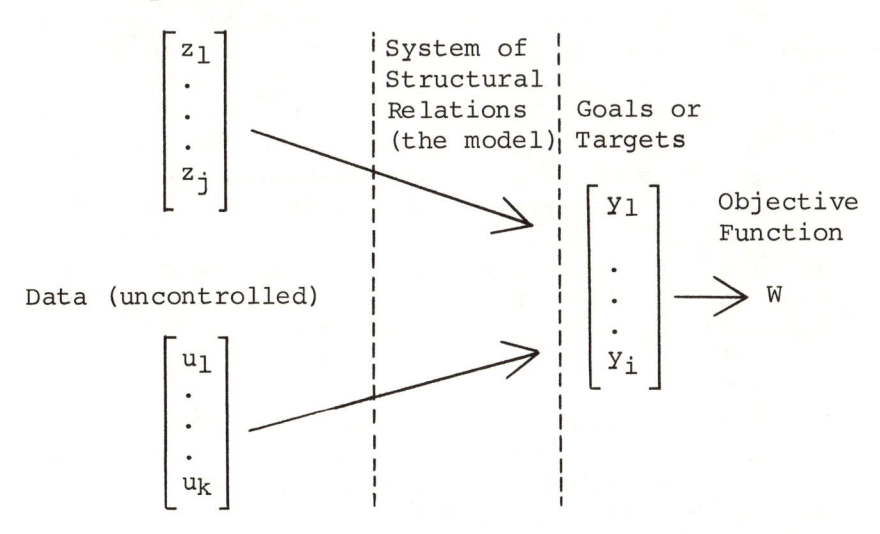

$$\begin{bmatrix} z_1 \\ \cdot \\ \cdot \\ \cdot \\ z_j \end{bmatrix} \xrightarrow{\text{System of Structural Relations (the model)}} \begin{bmatrix} y_1 \\ \cdot \\ \cdot \\ \cdot \\ y_i \end{bmatrix} \xrightarrow{\text{Objective Function}} W$$

Data (uncontrolled)

$$\begin{bmatrix} u_1 \\ \cdot \\ \cdot \\ \cdot \\ u_k \end{bmatrix}$$

$z_1 \ldots z_j$ = policy instruments

$u_1 \ldots u_k$ = historical data

$y_1 \ldots y_i$ = goals or targets

W = objective or preference function

The usual econometric model reads across this figure
to the column headed "Goals" and supplies estimates

of various projections to the policy-maker. This corresponds to the set of projections mentioned earlier. Once having combined policy instruments such as government investment, tax rates, and export policies with historical data through regression analysis, certain combinations of these policies are specified and their effects on the target variables are noted. Algebraically, the model in the figure can be written in structural terms, as follows:

$$Ay = Bz + Cu \qquad (1)$$

If $\underline{A}$ is square and nonsingular, one can solve for the reduced form of the structural equations:

$$y = A^{-1}Bz + A^{-1}Cu \qquad (2)$$

This is the traditional formulation. By varying some stated set of policies z_j, one can then project its impact on the target variables y_i. There is no assurance, however, unless an overwhelming knowledge of the underlying structure by the analyst is posited, that an optimal set of policy instruments has been chosen. There is always the possibility that some other set of policies, given the interrelations in the structure of the model, would have given a more desirable combination of target variables. By restructuring the problem in an economic-policy framework, this problem is hopefully alleviated.

If it is possible to derive the structural coefficients in (1) from the reduced-form coefficients in (2), then the structural system can be solved for some set of optimal policies:

$$z = B^{-1}Ay - B^{-1}Cu \qquad (3)$$

It is also possible to derive (3) directly by estimating the structural equations by two-stage least squares, but the actual method of estimation has not been definitively decided upon. In any case, $\underline{z}$ in (3) will be an optimal policy set to the extent that the model is accurate and to the extent that the notions as to the components of $\underline{y}$ are correct. The notation $\underline{y}$ is some vector of targets that are weighted in some manner. To discover the targets and the weights, some information is needed about $\underline{W}$ in the figure, which represents the objective function of policy-makers.

To the extent that this objective function has a single component, such as maximizing the gross national product (GNP), there is no particular problem. But, if this were the valid characterization of the objective function, regional development agencies would most likely not be in existence. The body politic and the existence of various checks and balances have assured that other goals will be considered in addition to national economic efficiency, defined as growth in the GNP. The exact nature of the components and the weights of the objective function for Coastal Zone management is, of course, what the authors are trying to derive in the research procedure described above. The work on econometric models and on objective-setting is viewed as mutually supporting, with the models providing information useful in developing alternative development strategies and statements of goals and with the goals statements (in objective-function form) providing input data for use in the econometric model to derive an "optimal" policy set.

SUMMARY

In summary, the authors believe that policy-making for the Coastal Zone and its resources should start with a conscious attempt to define goals for the region, for systems analysis and detailed planning techniques for the region will be effective only if they can proceed from a well-developed set of goals. It is not intended that the goals statement become merely an "apple pie and motherhood" exercise; there are some real choices to be made.

If this approach differs from Schoop's experience in planning for the San Francisco Bay area, as described in Chapter 1, above, it is because not all desired uses of the Coastal Zone are compatible. Some trade-offs will be made between economic development and environmental protection, or even between alternative modes of economic development. It is important to recognize this fact and to deal with it explicitly in setting goals before beginning to talk about trade-offs in specific projects. A goals statement for the entire region will help to put particular projects in context. It may help alert people to particular problems or dangers for the entire zone and prevent them from focusing too narrowly on individual environmental crises.

It is interesting in this context to look at proposed national legislation for Coastal Zone management, as reported by Adams in Chapter 2, above. The administration proposal (H.R. 14845) has a statement of national interest in "effective management, beneficial use, protection and development of the land and water resources of the Nation's estuaries and coastal zones." This statement in itself allows both protection and development.

Subsequent statements stress the ecological and natural values of the zones, however, and hold that "continued unplanned and uncoordinated development pose an immediate threat of irreversible harm to the coastal zone for which the citizens of all of the States have an interest." This appears to state that the national interest is best served by controlling development so that it does no irreversible harm to the natural ecosystem. Yet the bill provides considerable latitude to the states to develop programs that meet the special requirements of their coastal areas. In effect, the question of precise formulation of the objective function and preparation of management strategies is left to the states. This underscores the importance of the research that the authors propose to do.

Aside from the econometric-model approach, nothing has been said about systems-analysis models--especially those that portray the physical behavior of the Coastal Zone. These production-functions models, digital or analog, simulation or mathematical programing, are, of course, very useful in tracing through the consequences of management programs for estuaries and Coastal Zones. The authors view their research as contributing to a systems approach in which these models play an important role.

The term "development and management strategy" has been chosen to describe a set of management policies and programs that would be dynamic in nature. That is, investments and management programs would be scheduled over time and would be modified as results of previous actions became available and as conditions, both from within and from outside the region, change. Flexibility--the ability to change programs and policies without great losses--would be built into the strategies. There would be need for timely analysis and evaluation of programs in terms of how they contribute to meeting the objectives, and environmental monitoring and basic data programs would be required to strike a set of "environmental accounts" to go along with economic and social accounts for the region. Such programs of monitoring and accounting can best be developed if Coastal Zone managers have clear and specific notions of the important objectives to be pursued and their relative importance.

The approach described here is tentative. Major changes will probably be made as research proceeds. Perhaps the scope of some of the proposed research will have to be reduced. But the authors propose to hold to the basic principle of applying one version of the rational-planning and decision-making approach to the complicated problem setting of the Coastal Zone.

NOTES

1. See Anitni Etzoni, "Mixed Scanning: A 'Third' Approach to Decision Making, "Public Administration Review, XXVII, 5 (December, 1967), 385-92; Charles E. Lindblom, The intelligence of Democracy: Decision Making Through Mutual Adjustment (New York: The Free Press, 1965); and Aaron Wildavsky, "The Political Economy of Efficiency, Cost-Benefit Analysis, Systems Analysis and Program Budgeting," Public Administration

Review, XXVI, 4 (December, 1966), 292-310.

    2. See Leonard Lecht, National Planning Association, Goals, Priorities, and Dollars: The Next Decade (New York: The Free Press, 1966); and Robert C. Young, "Goals and Goal-Setting," Journal of the American Institute of Planners, XXXII, 2 (March, 1966) 76-85.

    3. Goals for Americans (Englewood Cliffs, N.J.: Prentice-Hall, 1960), report of the President's Commission on National Goals.

    4. Regional Plan Association, Goals for the Region (New York, 1963).

    5. Goals for Dallas (Dallas, Texas, 1966).

ANALYSIS
by John Kissin

THE NEED FOR FLEXIBILITY

This analysis will focus on two aspects of environmental planning--flexibility and data needs. At one time, the term "flexibility" was almost as popular in the planning field as "change" is today. The two concepts are connected. Flexibility can be interpreted as a means of allowing for unforeseen change or, rather, as an investment by which extra expenditures are incurred now in order to reduce the expenditures that will have to be incurred to accommodate future changes that cannot be foreseen. There are three main kinds of changes that can occur and that are likely to force a change in plans: changes in society's knowledge about the world in which it wishes to operate, changes in the technology at its disposal, and changes in the goals and objectives that it sets for itself and in the things that it thinks are important.

An example of the first kind of change is that of knowledge of the importance of tidal marshes. For a long time, these were regarded as a nuisance, to be dredged or filled as soon as this seemed economically feasible. It is only since the 1960's or sooner that there has been a general recognition that salt marshes are something that ought perhaps to be preserved. A long-term plan made in 1960 or 1965 would have envisaged eliminating most of them, and a long-term statement of goals at that time might well have described their elimination or economic development as an objective.

An example of the second kind of change lies in the still hypothetical development of what may be called electronic shopping. Some writers envision the time, in the fairly near future, when housewives will make their selections from supermarket shelves by means of closed-circuit television from their own kitchens; and the payments will be charged to their bank account automatically. Plainly, such a development would have considerable impact on the land requirements for stores, for parking, and maybe for travel. It is impossible to tell now whether this is a reasonable prediction, or whether electronic shopping will go the way of the monorail and the backyard helicopter. Should one plan on the assumption that such a development will not occur, and risk having investments in conventional shipping centers wasted, or should one plan on the assumption that it will occur, and risk having to fit shopping centers into a land-use pattern that has been planned on the assumption that they will become superfluous? In a case like this, where there seems to be some knowledge of the alternatives, a game-theoretic analysis may lead to a rational decision.

An example of the third kind of change lies in the increasing importance that is attached to environmental pollution. Many people will be familiar with Ebenezer Howard's Garden Cities of Tomorrow, in which he described what he hoped would become a form of urban environment that was superior to anything then available for the majority of the population.[1] His proposed layout for these "garden cities" was a circular plan, with commerce at the core, surrounded by residential areas, and industry distributed around the edge. What Howard overlooked was that this scheme was certain to leave the residential areas affected by industrial pollution, irrespective of which way the wind was blowing. The point was not that Howard was indifferent to environmental quality (if he had been, he would not have written his book), but that air pollution was then a pretty minor problem

A POLICY ANALYSIS APPROACH

compared to the ones he was dealing with, and he did not give it much thought.

LIMITATIONS OF LONG-RANGE PLANNING

The strong likelihood of unforseeable changes means that long-range planning is a somewhat dubious procedure. Long-range plans have to be made, but one should do so in the knowledge that they will probably have to be changed. The formulation of long-range goals seems to be equally dubious, and much less necessary. There is no way of knowing what the goals of 1975 or 1980 will be, but one thing is pretty sure--some of them will involve cleaning up the mess made in pursuit of the goals of 1970. That is all right though. If present planning is doing its job, that means that the problems being created for the future will be less serious than the problems being solved. As long as men are not infallible, that is about the best one can hope for, and, in general, that seems to be the way things are working out. But, if an attempt is made to institutionalize long-range social goals, then the correction of mistakes will become more difficult.

If Hufschmidt and his colleagues had carried out their research in 1960 or 1965, their goals would have probably implied commercial and industrial development of the coastline to a much greater extent than would now be considered wise. If such goals had been formally adopted by government at that time, it would not have eliminated the present divisiveness about coastal development; it would just have made the correction of earlier mistakes even harder than it is anyhow. As long as economic resources are scarce, there is likely to be some conflict about their distribution. Thus, the hope of eliminating future conflicts once and for all by the formulation of social goals seems wholly illusory. The author tends to agree with the views that Hufschmidt and his colleagues have attributed to Lindblom and others --that any attempt to state a set of social goals at the outset of an investigation is doomed to failure.

Rather than spend time in trying to formulate an objective function for policy planning, it would be better to try to improve knowledge of the con-constraints. Just what sets of activities are compatible? Exactly what would have to be given up in the way of recreation, fishing, and so forth, if the BASF chemical plant were built in Beaufort County, South Carolina? What would be the consequences to the natural system if it were built on, say, the Savannah River or the Ashley River, as some have suggested? At present, there are only the haziest of ideas about how to set about answering questions like this.

DATA NEEDS

The main difference between the planning of the moon shot and the planning of Coastal Zone development probably lies in the lack of data for the latter, rather than in the lack of an agreed objective function. Most of the elements that are used in the spacecraft are man-made, and presumably somebody knows how they work and how they interact. By contrast, it is not known how the elements of the natural system interact, and no one is too clear on how the economic and social system, which can also be regarded as being man-made in a sense, operates. It is this lack of data that prevents the country from repeating the success of the Apollo program. It is not that people do not know what they want to do as much as that they have not much more than the faintest idea of how to do it. Therefore, the primary objective of research should be to find out more about the nature and operation of the systems that people are trying to deal with.

Some researchers, who have little or no background in biology or ecology, have been trying to glean numbers from the published literature that could begin to yield some first approximations to a lower boundary on the economic costs arising from changes to the natural system that result from economic development of the Coastal Zones. Such numbers are needed not only if Knetsch's proposed

A POLICY ANALYSIS APPROACH

pricing mechanism is to be instituted but also if any estimate of trade-offs between alternative uses of natural resources is to be made. Economists are simply not qualified to gather or evaluate this kind of data, and, hopefully, those who are better qualified will be able to see their way to helping to obtain this information.

One can understand the reluctance of ecologists and marine biologists to be more forthright about the quantitative implications of coastal policy decisions. In the first place, they are naturally reluctant to commit themselves to numbers at a time when the empirical justification for a particular number may be weak. In the second place, any detailed figure they may give is liable to be misused for purposes of political controversy. Even so, one would like some data on the effects of, say, filling a particular salt marsh other than such that will lead to the apocalypse. It may be that the ecosystem is so delicately balanced that any further interference is liable to lead to the collapse of the entire "life-support system," as many ecologists suggest. But most people are skeptical of a proposition like this and would need to have much more detailed and specific evidence of it before being willing to act on it.

The failure of the power structure to respond to pleas such as the one heard from ecologists is probably not due to lack of concern over the environment. The policies that have led to the present situation cannot reasonably be attributed to the Judeo-Christian ethic alone; the ancient Romans had their problems resulting from overexploitation of natural resources--think of the deforestation of the Apennines. Nor can the present ecological crisis be blamed on the prevailing individualist philosphy of this country; the Soviet Government has become seriously concerned with the pollution of Lake Baikal in recent years but has not yet found a way of solving the problem. The crisis, if it is a crisis, is a result of past ignorance and can only be remedied by enlightenment--not by impassioned warnings about the imminent end of life on earth (although such warnings may be justified)--by a precise, and as far as possible quantitative, exposition of the reasoning that has led to any conclusions that ecologists have reached.

NOTE

1. See Ebenezer Howard, Garden Cities of Tommorrow, ed. F. J. Osborn (Cambridge, Mass.: The M.I.T. Press, 1965), originally published in 1902.

CHAPTER 7

ECOLOGICAL CONSIDERATIONS
by Arthur W. Cooper

Up to this point, only man's institutions and the role they have to play in the development of a rational system of management for the Coastal Zone have been considered here. No one can deny that any management system is, ultimately, a system that blends economic theory, law, and politics into a program that is theoretically sound, legally workable, and at least palatable from a political point of view. The most vital element has not yet been considered, however, for no one has even begun to involve environmental considerations in the development of a management system.

Such an arrangement, in a sense, mirrors the fallacy of man's thinking up to this time with respect to management practices in the Coastal Zone. He has thought first about that which is profitable from an economic point of view, second about that which might be politically palatable, and only lately about the legal implications of what he has done. Last of all, he considers the environment--the ecology of the Coastal Zone. Society's priorities have been reversed and that reversal has been perpetuated here.

Resource management is only one of the elegant

games that man plays. It differs, however, from many of his other games because the stakes are higher. His future survival and well-being are the stakes. In playing any game, one must know all of the players and the ways that they can influence the outcome of the game. If one attempts to develop a system of management for the Coastal Zone that does not first take into account the basic ecology of the Coastal Zone, the system is doomed to failure.
Nature is the most powerful player in the game, and it dictates the tempo and rules by which the game is played. By studying nature, one can learn the strategy by which he can successfully remain a player in the game.

This paper will review those ecological facts that the author considers vital to an understanding of the Coastal Zone and will show how these facts are relevant to any system of management for the Coastal Zone.

BASIC ECOLOGICAL CONSIDERATIONS IN THE COASTAL ZONE

The Coastal Zone is that region where land and fresh water, on the one hand, meet salty ocean water, on the other. The term "estuary" is often used for this region and, for the purposes of this discussion, the two terms will be considered to be virtually synonymous, although it should be realized that the term "Coastal Zone" is potentially much wider in scope, including not only estuaries but also beaches (coasts) and continental-shelf waters.

The Coastal Zone in one physiographic region is different from that in another area. Along the South Atlantic Coast, fragile, sandy beaches protect the mouths of rivers, the estuaries, and the shoreline proper. Natural stands of vegetation tie the sand strands together and protect the Coastal Zone from the effects of the open sea. Marshes fringe the estuary and serve as nursery areas for many fish and shellfish that enter from the open sea. Much food material produced in the marshes is washed out on

ECOLOGICAL CONSIDERATIONS

the tides and becomes a major part of the energy budget of the larger Coastal Zone system. Tidal mudflats, with their communitites of buried shellfish and worms, rely, to a large extent, on food materials produced elsewhere. Floating water plants and animals, the plankton, contain many of the juvenile forms of valued fish and shellfish species and occupy the shallow, well-lighted waters of the estuary.

Perhaps the most fundamental concept of ecology is that which holds that nature consists of a series of ecosystems (ecological systems)--natural, man-influenced, and man-made. Each of these systems consists of interrelated populations of plants and animals, flows of water and energy, and invisible pathways through which both essential and nonessential nutrients are cycled. These systems may exist on various scales of size and complexity. The Coastal Zone consists of an array of ecological systems, such as marshes, mudflats, shallow open water, mud and sand bottom, beaches, and dunes. Each of these systems has its own characteristics plants and animals, and each has evolved in such a way that it has a characteristic pattern of energy flow and nutrient cycling.

The ecological systems of the Coastal Zone, although possessing their own discrete properties, are coupled together in such a way that the entire region consists of a series of discrete, yet interdependent, systems. The activities of one system clearly influenced the functioning of other systems in the area. This is shown by the movement of nutrient substances in an estuarine system, such as the mouth of a major river. Nutrients wash down the river from the upland, collecting from an entire drainage system. Some of these may be used by plankton floating in the open waters of the estuary. Many of those that are not used by plankton are bound into the tissues of marsh plants and "fed back" into the estuary slowly by bacterial action after the plants die.

Thus, the nutrients moving into the estuary from the upland become rather evenly dispersed throughout the estuary and move through many of the smaller ecosystems found within the larger estuarine system.

Because of the clearly interrelated nature of coastal ecosystems, it logically follows that phenomena that alter a single ecosystem may produce effects that are observed widely throughout a number of other systems.

There is another dimension to this "openness" of coastal ecosystems. Not only are estuarine systems themselves interrelated, but they are also intimately related to the systems found in ocean waters on the continental shelf near the land. Nutrient materials flushed from the land move through the Coastal Zone and are utilized by nearshore systems. Many fish species inhabiting the continental shelf either migrate into the estuary to reproduce or have young forms that do so. Thus, the Coastal Zone must be expanded in people's thinking to include not only ecosystems of the estuary proper but also those systems of the continental slopes that are tied to the Coastal Zone.

One of the most interesting ecological facts to emerge from recent research concentrated on the Coastal Zone is the very high rates of productivity characteristic of estuarine ecosystems. On a relative scale, these systems rank among the most productive of temperate ecosystems and, in absolute terms, the annual rates of energy fixation in several systems approach those found for the most productive ecosystems on earth, such as tropical rain forests.

A number of factors combine to produce these high productivities.[1] The different systems of the estuary, such as marshes, mud communities, and plankton, make maximum use of the available environmental resources, such as light and nutrients. Tidal movement contributes to high productivity by regularly increasing the surface area under which phytoplankton may grow and by serving as a means for transporting materials throughout the estuary. Decomposing organic matter may thus be transported from an area of excess production, such as a marsh, to an area where production is limited, such as a tidal mudflat. Furthermore, tidal action continually supplies fresh nutrients to estuarine systems, thus ensuring a maximal

ECOLOGICAL CONSIDERATIONS

rate of growth. Finally, the feeding habits of many estuarine animals and microorganisms produce a rapid rate of nutrient regeneration and ensure maximum conservation of nutrients within the estuary. These high rates of estuarine productivity clearly are the biological basis for the abundant life of the Coastal Zone, upon which man so heavily depends.

Estuarine systems are adapted to environmental change, for change is one of the facts of life of the Coastal Zone. Many systems are programed for regular, cyclic changes, such as the tides. Species of plants and animals have features of their activity--such as seed germination, feeding, and reproduction--geared to tidal movements. Annual environmental changes may produce dramatic changes in community structure and function. K. R. Tenore, for example, has found that an annual cycle occurs in the Pamlico River, in North Carolina, in which dissolved oxygen in the deeper parts of the river drops to zero during late summer and fall.[2] These anoxic conditions cause an almost complete destruction of the macrobenthic fauna of the deep-river sediments. Wind-driven circulation in the fall restores oxygen to the deeper waters, and larvae enter from the sound during winter and spring, thus re-establishing the benthic community.

Catastrophies may also exert dramatic, and long-term, effects on coastal systems. Hurricanes and northeasters may destroy or alter vast stretches of the beach and dune ecosystem. Under calmer conditions, however, conditions may be restored and a new equilibrium may be established. Many Coastal Zone ecosystems, in fact, possess characteristics of early successional communities because they have relatively low diversities of species and because the ultimate dominants of the community become established as pioneers. In this way, estuarine systems are adapted both to regular and to catastrophic change.

MAN'S INTERACTIONS WITH COASTAL ZONE ECOSYSTEMS

Any consideration of ecology of the Coastal Zone must take into account man's past and present interaction with the ecosystems of the zone. From these past interactions, an effective initial model for a Coastal Zone management system can be developed. Man subjects coastal ecosystems to a number of direct modifications, or stresses, whose effects are immediately apparent.[3] These involve activities ranging from development of building sites, through industrial activity, to commercial and sports fishing.

Perhaps the most serious modification involves the direct loss of estuarine areas by bulkheading and filling of productive shallow areas. In this case, what are often the most productive estuarine lands are removed forever by filling to a level above the high-tide line. This construction often accompanies, or is a by-product of, dredging for navigation purposes. Dredging, or other changes in configuration of the estuary, frequently produce changes in the pattern of water circulation, thus limiting exchanges between the various subsystems of the estuary.

Similarly, upstream diversions of fresh water by dams or diversion canals may produce dramatic changes in the normal pattern of sediment or nutrient input into the estuary. In some cases, as in Charleston Harbor, diversions have introduced massive new loads of sediment that, ultimately, produce rapid shoaling. In other cases, diversions of nutrients may radically reduce the nutrient input into estuarine systems, causing a reduction in the productivity of the systems.

Industrial and agricultural activity adds large quantities of pollutants, either in the form of increased loads of naturally occurring substances (such as nitrogen or phosphorus) or in the form of toxic materials (such as lead or pesticides). These substances may produce a host of large-scale or subtle effects. Toxic substances may accumulate in organisms occupying relatively high positions in food chains, or they may produce marked changes in the physiological functioning of susceptible organisms. Finally, biological imbalances may occur as a result of selective overexploitation of valuable species, from the selective effects of certain toxic substances or from ill-advised introductions of exotic species. As indicated, all of these effects are rather immediate and dramatic, and thus the "remedy," at least in ecological terms, is rather apparent.

Conversely, many of man's effects may be much more subtle.[4] These effects may occur over long periods of time, and the original stress may thus be difficult to determine. For example, recent studies have revealed that, when a system is subjected to limited stresses over long periods of time, there is a gradual reduction in species diversity. This effect is greatest in systems adapted to relatively constant environmental conditions and is least in systems that are programed to survive constantly recurring environmental stresses.

Another subtle effect resulting from continued application of stress is a reduction in the length of food chains. This is a logical outcome of a reduction in total system diversity and may be related to the need for the community to shunt its total energy use from complexity of transfer pattern to simple survival. The system responds to the added energy drain, in the form of a stress, by abbreviating energy transfer so that it takes place through fewer trophie levels. Wohlschlag and Copeland further point out that continued stress may produce pronounced declines in population numbers through sublethal effects on the physiology of organisms that may be very difficult to detect.[5]

A COASTAL ZONE MANAGEMENT SYSTEM WITH AN ECOLOGICAL BASIS

The basic thesis of this paper is that any system of management devised for the Coastal Zone must, as a _first_ consideration, reflect the ecological processes that occur in that zone. These basic natural forces and processes form, in a sense, the constraints within which a management system must be developed. If it develops outside these constraints or fails to take them into consideration, it will fail.

Clearly, any management system must also take into account political and social constraints as well; but, when concessions are made, they must be made in favor of natural processes, not in favor of man-oriented processes. This may sound naive, but a moment's reflection will indicate this to be the only path that may safely be taken if the Coastal Zone resources that are prized so much and that are so necessary to continued welfare of the country are to be protected.

Inasmuch as the Coastal Zone consists of a series of closely related ecosystems, each dependent upon the other in various ways, it logically follows that the management system should look at the Coastal Zone as a whole, not in terms of limited portions. An estuary must be viewed as a natural unit, and its management must be planned for as a unit, not in piecemeal fashion, as in the past. Such planning obviously does not come easily.

Throughout most of this country, decision-making regarding resource use has usually been left to the smallest ultimate political unit, the county. In a few limited cases, basin-wide or estuary-wide planning has been attempted. Local governments will not easily give up their authority in the planning and zoning field, for it is through these tools that the local unit regulates its growth and development. Perhaps the answer to the dilemma is to divide each state into a limited number of natural units, analogous to river basins, and require the counties bordering such units to plan together for their management. The states and the federal government must clearly have back-up authority to develop management plans when lesser political units either have failed to act or have acted in a grossly unwise fashion.

Key elements of any such planning effort are inventories of the systems to be managed. It remains one of the great tragedies of ecology that knowledge about natural systems is so spotty. Much is known about the function of some coastal systems, and virtually nothing is known about the function of others. Further, systematic inventories of natural

ECOLOGICAL CONSIDERATIONS

resources are almost unknown in the United States. No one has ever paid careful attention to vegetation and resource-mapping in the way that European ecologists have. Such "description" is disdained, yet it forms the heart of any sane resource-management program.

As an intital step in any management program, the kinds of systems present in the landscape unit to be managed, as well as their distribution, must be determined, and what is known of their ecology must then be summarized. At the same time that this inventory is being made, existing land-use patterns, industrial uses, and political and legal authorities in the area must also be inventoried. These are the pieces that provide the framework around which the plan is drawn.

As a next step in developing the management plan, an approximation of the relative and absolute values of each of the natural and man-influenced systems in the Coastal Zone area that is to be managed must be developed. This determination of value should take several forms. First of all, the relative values of the roles that the various systems play in the estuary itself should be determined, as far as possible. Which systems are the most important in terms of production of basic food materials? Which systems are vital for fish and shellfish breeding? Which systems play a vital role in nutrient regeneration within the estuary? Which systems protect the others from natural destructive forces? Once these intersystem values are determined, the entire estuary may then be viewed in terms of the roles that the various subsystems play in the functioning of the larger system.

Second, an attempt should be made to express the value of estuarine systems in absolute terms; i.e., in terms of some unit of currency that has meaning in man's economic framework. This is a very difficult, and perhaps virtually impossible, task. It is clear that, when values associated with the functioning of natural systems are reduced to dollars, this can only be done in very general terms. Furthermore, many of the very vital functions that natural systems play cannot be reduced to dollar values. This does not mean that the natural system is not of value to man. It simply means that its values cannot be reduced to some common denominator with which man is familiar.

Recently, H. T. Odum has suggested that units of energy, such as the calorie, serve as a common denominator for relating natural systems to man's economic system.[6] Odum reasons that the calorie can be expressed in terms of dollar equivalents; in fact, he suggests that 10,000 kilocalories of energy are "worth" one 1970 U.S. dollar. Thus, if the work done by a natural community can be determined, it can then be translated into dollars.

Such computations, when applied to a 12,000-acre North Carolina coastal island, suggest that the "value" of the island approaches $50 million per year and that to replace it (by computing the energy expended to develop natural ecosystems to their present state of complexity) would cost a staggering $1.3 billion. Clearly, such computations are limited in their applicability, but at least they represent a first crude effort to reduce natural and man-made values to a common denominator.

Yet a third sort of value that must be assessed for natural systems is their contribution to man's life-support systems. These are values that are so profound and basic that people tend to take them for granted. For example, what is the value of coastal ecosystems in terms of oxygen production, in terms of effects on climate, or in terms of buffering capacity for absorbing storm energy? Although very difficult to assess, these things must at least be considered when the painful decisions are made about the relative value of natural ecosystems.

Many ecologists have argued that such an assessment described above is not possible because the ecological knowledge necessary to make such decisions is simply lacking. In part, this is true; however, it does not logically follow from this that one should not use what information he does have to arrive at a first approximation of ecological values. Many ecologists argue that, because the basic ecological data are not available, decisions cannot be made about values and that the first job, therefore, is to gather further basic data. Many more years must be spent, they say, in becoming informed about the details of system function before enough basic ecological data will exist to make rational decisions.

There are two reasons why this view is incorrect. The first of these is purely pragmatic and is based on the simple proposition that, if the information that is available now is not used to develop environmental management systems, then the management systems will be developed, but without any ecological input. The past has shown the danger of resource decision-making without ecological inputs. This situation cannot be perpetuated for any reason.

The second reason for believing that people must make do with what data they have is that this is basically the process that is followed in any decision-making process. All the information that is available is evaluated, and then one decides how best to manage. The system chosen is then continually modified as a result of new information that comes to light. As far as the Coastal Zone is concerned, a first approximation of a management program must be developed on the basis of the information that is available now. The program must be flexible so that it can be adjusted in the light of new data, as they are brought forth. New data must constantly be sought, but ecologists cannot abdicate their role in the planning process simply because every last datum is not known about the functioning of every estuarine system. Enough is known to paint the broad picture; the details can and will follow afterward.

Once the system interactions are documented and values are established, the next step in developing a management program is the allocation of use status to estuarine lands and waters. This is the concept of landscape zoning that Eugene Odum has so eloquantly urged for the Coastal Zone.[7] As

Odum points out, it is nonsense to think that maximum efficient use of everything can be achieved on the same unit area of land. Certain land uses are incompatible. One cannot raise oysters and build houses on the same acre of shallow bottoms.

Somehow, a decision must be made about which use a given unit of Coastal Zone land is best suited for. As indicated above, these zoning decisions must be made by weighing ecological values against the values associated with other uses. Odum points out that these decisions may take two forms. On the one hand, one may opt for several compromise uses of the same unit area, recognizing that the result will be less than optimum returns for any given use. On the other hand, one may rigidly zone certain areas for particular purposes, always keeping in mind the interdependence of estuarine ecosystems.

The zoning decisions that must be made are clearly the most vital decisions in the development of any management plan. They must be made with full input from ecologists, as well as from local governmental officials, development authorities, economists, and planners. Opportunities for error obviously exist. The direction in which errors are made, however, is a vital consideration. From an ecological point of view, any management system that is developed must be conservative and must contain built-in allowances for the fact that the values of Coastal Zone ecosystems can be estimated only imperfectly.

In other words, if a mistake is made, it must be conservative and in favor of natural ecosystems and functions, rather than in favor of man's alterations of such systems. For example, if the amount of salt marsh that must be preserved in order to maintain a healthy fishery is overestimated, then the protection criteria can always be relaxed, and additional modification of those areas judged to be of least importance can be permitted. If a mistake is made in the opposite direction and an adequate amount of salt marsh is not protected, however, when this is realized, it will be too late to take corrective measures. The fishery resource will be seriously jeopardized and society will be literally powerless to take steps to remedy the situation.

The necessity to err in favor of nature and natural processes is a pill that many nonecologists find too bitter to swallow. They argue that failure to utilize resources now retards the rate of economic growth. The ecologist argues, however, that it is precisely this attitude that has gotten the country into environmental trouble. If one errs conservatively, and in favor of nature, one preserves options for future generations. If one errs against nature, one closes out one's options all too rapidly.

The final step in development of the management plan consists of translation into political reality--selling the program to the people. It is trite to say that, without success in this area, the entire program will fail. In the case of a management program that contains as one of its major elements restrictions on land use, however, there must be strong acceptance by the general public or the program will fail.

Traditionally, coastal people have been unwilling to accept limitations on the use of their lands and waters, and one may expect that many of them will approach any program of zoning with the same jaundiced view. Therefore, the reasons for the program, the ecological bases for the land-use restrictions that are proposed, must be very carefully explained and justified. One must be optimistic that, with a careful job of explanation, wide public acceptance of the needed restrictions can be achieved. In view of the strong cultural tradition that estuarine resources are common-property resources, optimism seems justified.[8]

Whatever management system ultimately evolves for the Coastal Zone, it will certainly be a mix of man and nature, of natural ecological systems and man's social systems. As an ecologist, the plea of the author is that, through all stages of development, planning involve ecological reasoning. If it does not, the management plans will be no better than those of the past, which have led to the present environmental crisis in the Coastal Zone.

NOTES

1. C. L. Schelske and H. T. Odum, "Mechanisms Maintaining High Productivity in Georgia Estuarines," Proceedings of the 14th Session, Gulf and Caribbean Fisheries Institute, Miami, Florida, 1961, pp. 75-80.

2. K. R. Tenore, *Macrobenthos of the Pamlico River, N.C., Estuary*, Ph.D. thesis, (Raleigh, N.C.: North Carolina State University, 1970).

3. D. E. Wohlschlag and B. J. Copeland, "Fragile Estuarine Systems--Ecological Considerations," *Water Resources Bulletin* 6: 94-105.

4. *Ibid.*

5. *Ibid.*

6. Schelske and Odum, *op. cit.*

7. E. P. Odum, "Estuarine Agriculture," Proceedings of a Symposium on Estuaries Ecology, North Carolina Water Resources Research Institute, Raleigh, N.C., 1966, pp. 62-64.

8. E. A. Laurent and J. C. Hite, "Resource Management in the Coastal Zone: The Policy Problem," in "Economics of Marine Resources 3," (Clemson, S.C.: South Carolina Agricultural Experiment Station, 1970).

ANALYSIS
by Norbert Dee

The paper presented by Cooper is a valuable contribution here because it clearly states why and how one should include the necessary ecological considerations in the total management of the Coastal Zone. Too often a discussion on the importance of ecology in a management context digresses into an emotional appeal on the merits of ecology and is not based on sound scientific principles; that was not the case with Cooper's presentation.

In his paper, he has stated the importance of treating the entire Coastal Zone as a system consisting of various components, such as tidal mudflats, marshes, beaches, and shallow open water. These components, in turn, are related to the productivity of the Coastal Zone, on which man is dependent. He has also indicated what effects dredging, fresh-water diversions, and industrial and municipal pollution have had on the ecology of the Coastal Zone. In order to avoid major ecological problems in the future, he has suggested that a four-step approach be included in the management program. This approach would consist of an inventory of the ecosystems present in the Coastal Zone, an approximation of the relative and absolute value of each component in the system, a zoning of the Coastal Zone into various uses, and the selling of the ecological program to the people.

Instead of further restating what has been

adequately expressed by Cooper, the author will divide his comments into two parts: a discussion of some of the specific approaches expressed in Cooper's paper and some additional comments on a method that could be used to analyze the various environmental alternatives in the Coastal Zone. The latter comments are an extension of remarks that were made by Cooper.

DISCUSSION

Cooper states that the management system that evolves will be a mix of natural ecological systems and man's social systems. This concept of a multiple-objective management system must be restated in order to emphasize its importance. In the past, most decisions were based only on economic considerations such as income, increased production, regional or national growth, and so forth. The only time that environmental or social considerations were included in the analysis was when a dollar value could be put on these benefits or costs and therefore included in the benefit-cost ratio. The effect on the environment and on society in general as a result of those single-purpose decisions is being felt in the Coastal Zone today. Therefore, in future decisions, it is important to make sure that the decision process is based on multiple-objective criteria.

This multiple-objective approach to a Coastal Zone management system cannot be obtained, as Cooper realistically suggests, by proposing that no "environmental concessions" be made in any management decision. It must be remembered that, in many cases, the goals of economic growth and environmental preservation or enhancement are not competitive, and, therefore, there is no real problem. But, if a conflict arises, what is needed is a decision process that evaluates both the economic and the environmental component and selects the alternative that "best" satisfies both criteria. It is obvious that, in this type of multiple-objective decision, certain "environmental concessions" will have to be made in order to obtain this desired mix. Given this situation, environmental quality can best be maintained or improved by helping the decision-maker select those concessions that have a minimal effect on the environment, instead of saying that no concessions should be made.

In step two of his management plan, Cooper suggests that an approximation of the relative and absolute values of each natural and man-influenced system be developed and used to select between various alternatives. This is a very important suggestion, and will be commented upon later in the paper. He also suggests, however, that a monetary value be put on both the natural and the man-influenced systems. To date there have been no successful dollar analyses of either type of system. The reason for this problem is that the environmental resources are not explicitly traded in the market place and, therefore, have no real dollar value in use or in exchange. Thus, when it becomes necessary to put a value on the resource, only a minimum intrinsic value, arbitrarily chosen by the evaluator, can usually be estimated, and, therefore, in any comparison of benefits and costs, the benefits are understated, if the benefit-cost analysis can be achieved at all.

If it is necessary to approximate these benefits, the approximation should be based on a measurement of society's willingness to pay for the preservation of the environment and not as suggested by Cooper by transforming energy units into dollar values. Also implied in the use of total energy as a measurement is that the subsystems of food production, breeding, regeneration, and environmental protection can be completely expressed in a common unit of measurement and that their interrelationships can also be expressed in that unit. This seems to be an important assumption that should be explicitly stated in any evaluation procedure.

Because there is a real problem with putting dollar values on the environment and with the acceptability of a common unit of measurement, the environment should be evaluated separately from the evaluation of economic considerations in any management process. Thus, there would be at least two components that would be evaluated in a decision--the economic and the environmental. This approach was suggested in the preliminary report of the Water Resources Task Force.[1]

A PROPOSED METHOD OF ENVIRONMENTAL EVALUATION

At this point, the author would like to suggest a method that could be used to evaluate the environment. The technique is useful because the decision-maker would know not only the economic benefits from each of the various alternatives but also the corresponding environmental impact of each alternative. This would allow him to weight the environmental impact and the economic growth, and then select the "best" mix.

This evaluation procedure will include more than just the ecological considerations that were stated by Cooper. It will include the entire environment with which man interacts, both natural and man-made. There are four components to this definition that, in their own way, measure the impact of man's various interations with the system. They include the following elements:

1. Aesthetics, such as ocean views, wilderness areas, and natural undisturbed environment

2. Cultural significance, such as historically and educationally significant areas

3. Ecological systems (natural systems), as described by Cooper

4. Environmental quality, such as water, air, and land areas being free from pollution.

The evaluation procedure involves the relative weighting of each of the various alternatives that is being considered in a specific decision. That is, each alternative is evaluated as to its environmental impact by comparing it to the environmental criteria of aesthetics, culture, quality, and ecology. Each deviation from the desired goals is quantified by a number or index. For example, if an alternative lowered the dissolved oxygen of an estuary below 5 mg/l, the impact might be 9 on a scale of 10, where the higher the value, the greater the environmental impact. The sum of these indices or values represents the total environmental impact that would result if that alternative were selected. This process is continued until all the alternatives are evaluated and, therefore, an impact value is obtained that can be used to compare alternatives.[2]

The weights used in this evaluation procedure can be obtained with a technique called multidimensional scaling.[3] Briefly, multidimensional scaling can be defined as a systematic procedure by which subjective responses of individuals can be ranked and numerically weighted. In order to get the appropriate weights, a cross section of the individuals living in the Coastal Zone would be interviewed to determine the appropriate average to be used in the evaluation procedure. This cross section would consist of ecologists, economists, conservationists, developers, average citizens, politicians, and so forth. By allowing the individuals in the Coastal Zone to become involved in the evaluation process, it will be easier for them to understand and accept the final selection.

The result of this evaluation will be a list of possible alternative developments of the Coastal Zone, with each alternative having a benefit-cost ratio and an environmental-impact index. It will be easier for the decision-maker to evaluate the alternatives and to make a better decision. This approach is static in that the various individuals who supplied the input to the evaluation procedure cannot change their values for individual issues. In order to take this into account, a decision game is in the process of being developed to help the decision-maker choose between the various environmental and economic considerations and to see the results of his decision simulated over the next twenty years.[4]

The players in such a game could be a group of voting members of the Coastal Zone Commission. The Commission has the power to enact and enforce the environmental quality in the zone. The board members represent various constituencies in the zone such as conservationists, politicians, developers, and average citizens. Each player has differently defined attitudes toward pollution, economic growth, culture, recreation, and the like. These attitudes are defined as social utilities and are quantified through the use of a multidimensional-scaling technique. The game is played by having the board rule on various issues that might face a real government body. Each member has one vote, which he can use either to bargain with other members or to trade in turn for their vote on other issues. The final decision is reached by a majority vote of the board, which will then be used as an input to a simulation model to show to the board members the results of their decision.

In conclusion, in order to attain the goal that was stated by President Nixon, namely to preserve and enhance the environment, the environmental considerations must be included in the decision process.[5] Cooper's paper attempts to start the movement in that direction.

NOTES

1. "Procedures for Evaluation of Water and Related Land Resources Projects", (report to the Water Resources Council, Special Task Force, Washington, D.C., June, 1969).

2. See Frank G. Craighead, and John H. Craighead, "River Systems: Recreational Classification, Inventory, and Evaluation," *Naturalist*, XIII (Summer,

1962); and Luna Leopold, and Maura O'Brien Marchand, "On the Quantitative Inventory of the Riverscape," Water Resources Research, IV, 4 (August, 1968).

    3. See Peter C. Fishburn, "Methods of Estimating Additive Utilities," Management Science, XIII, 7 (March, 1967); and Warren S. Torgerson, Theory and Methods of Scaling, (New York: John Wiley & Sons, 1958).

    4. See Richard M. Davis, "Preliminary Report on a Water Pollution Control Game" (sponsored by the Center for Quantitative Science in Forestry, Fisheries, and Wildlife, University of Washington, Seattle, Washington, 1970).

    5. Richard M. Nixon, President's Message to Congress, February 10, 1970.

APPENDIXES

APPENDIX A

CORPS OF ENGINEERS
U.S. ARMY
NEWS RELEASE
ON REVISED NAVIGABLE
WATER PERMIT REGULATIONS

The Corps of Engineers announced today sweeping changes in its regulations pertaining to permits for work in navigable waterways. These changes, which were approved by Secretary of the Army, Stanley R. Resor, and the Chief of Engineers, Lieutenant General F. J. Clarke, require that greater emphasis be given to environmental values in evaluating permit applications.

The changes include:

--A statement that "The decision . . . will be based . . . on evaluation of the impact of the proposed work on the public interest." "Public interest" is described as including factors such as "navigation, fish and wildlife, water quality, economics, conservation, aesthetics, recreation, water supply, flood damage prevention, ecosystems, and, in general, the needs and welfare of the people." This change clarifies the standard against which permit applications are to be judged and re-emphasizes that the Corps is no longer concerned only with the impact that a proposed project may have on navigation.

--A new policy narrowing the function of harbor lines. The new regulations make it clear that harbor lines are merely guidelines for determining, with respect to the impact on navigation interests alone, the offshore limits of construction. Persons wishing to undertake work in navigable waters shoreward of harbor lines are now required to apply to the Corps for work permits. The previous regulations allowed riparian owners to erect open pile structures or to undertake solid-file construction shoreward of established harbor lines without obtaining a permit.

--A clarification of the responsibilities of the Corps of Engineers and the Department of the Interior with respect to offcoast oil-drilling operations. The new regulations note that the Department of the Interior is responsible for considering the impact that such operations may have on the total environment at the time of the selection of submerged lands of the Outer Continental Shelf for inclusion in the mineral-leasing program administered by the Department of the Interior but provide for consideration by the Corps of the "impact of the proposed work on navigation and national security."

--Revised regulations on the issuance of public notices and the holding of public hearings on permit applications. Except in cases involving minor work, where it is clear that the proposed work would have no significant impact on environmental values, notices containing information on the proposed work are to be posted in post offices or other public places and sent to a broadly defined list of affected interests. "Doubtful cases will be resolved in favor of public notice and normal processing." Interested parties are to be given a "reasonable time," defined as not less than thirty days except in emergency cases, to express their views. Public hearings are to be held whenever there is a manifestation of public interest in a permit application or whenever requested by federal, state, or local public authorities.

--A requirement that applicants not only define the areas they want to fill but also describe the type and location of structures proposed to be erected on the fill. Previously, applicants were not required to provide information concerning subsequent use of filled tracts.

--A requirement that applicants whose proposals involve outfall work must provide details on the character of the effluent, including chemical content, water-temperature differentials, toxins, sewage, type and quantity of suspended solids, amount and frequency of discharge, and the like, along with the proposed method of instrumentation and arrangements for bearing the expense of removal of solids. Before taking action on any such permit applications, the Corps' district engineers are required to consult with regional directors of the Department of the Interior and with federal and state agencies having water-pollution abatement responsibilities.

New permit forms for implementing the regulation changes have been furnished at Corps of Engineers field offices. Among other things, these forms stipulate that observance of regulations of the federal Water Quality Administration and state water-pollution control agencies are made a condition of the permit and that permittees must make every reasonable effort to carry out approved work in a manner that will minimize any adverse impact on fish, wildlife, and natural environmental values.

A special condition in permits authorizing the filling in of navigable waters restricts permittees from erecting buildings or structures not contemplated at the time of issuance of the permit or from significantly changing the outward appearance of approved structures or the use to which the filled tract is dedicated without first obtaining a permit modification. Such permittees are also required to maintain adequate records of the nature and frequency of discharges and to provide discharge information to the district engineer upon request.

APPENDIX

B

**DESCRIPTIONS OF
ILLUSTRATIVE STATE PROGRAMS
OF ESTUARINE CONSERVATION**

by Milton S. Heath, Jr.

EMPHASIS ON THE USE OF REGULATORY CONTROLS

Massachusetts

In addition to water-pollution control legislation, Massachusetts' principal regulatory controls for estuaries consist of (a) a statute prohibiting the removing, filling, or dredging of any bank, flat, marsh, meadow, or swamp bordering coastal waters, without specified local and state permission or restrictions;[1] and (b) a related statute authorizing a rule-making approach, under which the Commissioner of Natural Resources, with the approval of the Board of Natural Resources, may adopt regulations concerning alteration or pollution of coastal wetlands; if these regulations are found in court to constitute a "taking" of property, the Department of Natural Resources may proceed to condemn the land in fee or lesser interest by eminent domain.[2]

This legislation was enacted after extensive

---

*Parts of this Appendix are derived from an article to appear in <u>Land and Water Law Review</u>, "Estuarine Conservation Legislation in the States."

studies and reports. The Department of Natural Resources regards the rule-making authority as the more promising approach. It permits its department to move on a regional basis to preserve wetlands without waiting for actual development commitments. Under this law, for example, the Department of Natural Resources has established a wetlands protective area covering 8,000 acres on the North Shore of Massachusetts.

The Department of Natural Resources administers the program through several of its divisions. Program goals being carried out through a series of estuarine studies are to maintain the estuaries in as near as possible to present conditions, consistent with management programs. Estuarine research is currently supported at about $120,000. The conservation efforts are coordinated by the Department of Natural Resources, with the State Department of Public Works, the Division of Water Pollution Control, the Army Corps of Engineers, the Bureau of Commercial Fisheries, and the Bureau of Sports Fisheries.

The Massachusetts wetlands permit legislation has been sustained in lower court tests. A test case that reached the State Supreme Court was returned to the trial court for further findings.[3]

Maine

In addition to general water-pollution control and pesticide-control legislation, Maine's principal regulatory controls for estuarine protection involve (a) a 1967 coastal wetlands alternation permit law[4] and (b) Army Corps of Engineers permits for alteration of coastal wetlands. The 1967 wetland control law prohibits filling, removing, dredging, or draining of sanitary sewage into wetlands bordering coastal waters without a permit from the municipality (or county) affected, issued with the approval of the Wetlands Control Board. Approval may be withheld if the proposal threatens public health, safety, or welfare, would adversely affect abutting owners, or would damage conservation of water supplies, wildlife, or fisheries.

The 1970 Maine Legislature has enhanced the protection of estuarine and coastal waters by enacting laws that prohibit discharge of oil into coastal waters and that require all commercial or industrial development proposals that may substantially affect the environment to be approved by the State Environmental Improvement Commission.[5] Both the Department of Inland Fisheries and Game and the State Park Commission have current coastal land-acquisition programs. The U.S. Bureau of Sports Fisheries and Wildlife is acquiring about 4,000 acres of salt marsh as National Wildlife Refuge Areas.

The Wetlands Control Board consists of the Commissioner of Sea and Shore Fisheries, the Commissioner of Inland Fisheries and Game, the Forest Commissioner, the Chairman of the Highway Commission, and the Chairman of the Water Improvement Commission. The Department of Sea and Shore Fisheries has general responsibility for coastal fisheries. Land acquisition is a function of the Department of Inland Fisheries and Game (for water fowl) and the State Park Commission for recreational park purposes. Wetland acquisition for water-fowl purposes is proceeding at about $20,000 annually. Twenty-three miles of waterfront valued at $3 million are owned by the State Park Commission, and another $4 million in bond issues was authorized by the 10th Legislature.

North Carolina

To supplement the normal complement of regulatory controls and land-acquisition powers (including condemnation authority),[6] North Carolina in 1969 adopted a comprehensive estuarine legislative package embodying the recommendations of an interagency study committee. Laws were enacted to require permits for dredging or filling in the estuaries or in the state-owned lakes[7] and to prohibit littering of navigable waters or erection of signs or other structures in such waters without a permit.[8] A total of $500,000 was appropriated for state acquisition of high-priority estuarine lands identified by the interagency committee. In addition, $94,000 was appropriated to begin preparation of a long-range plan for estuarine conservation and management, and another $80,000 was appropriated to meet staffing needs for the augmented estuarine programs.

Administrative responsibility for estuarine functions in North Carolina is vested mainly in the Commissioner of Commercial and Sports Fisheries, a division head of the Department of Conservation and Development. The Commissioner's responsibilities are coordinated and, in some respects, shared with the Departments of Administration and of Water and Air Resources.

EMPHASIS ON LAND ACQUISITION

New Jersey

A large-scale estuarine acquisition effort is under way in New Jersey. Passage of a $60 million Green Acres bond issue in 1961 has reportedly resulted in acquisition of about 13,000 acres of salt marsh by the Division of Fish and Game, and another 10,000 acres are being acquired.[9] Previously, the Division of Fish and Game had acquired about 23,000 acres. The U.S. Bureau of Sport Fisheries and Wildlife expects to control over 50,000 acres when its acquisition plans are completed. Upon completion all of these programs, about 90 per cent of the high-value coastal salt marsh of New Jersey is expected to be protected. Under the Green Acres program, total state and local land acquisition in the coastal counties has been about 53,000 acres. An additional 10,000 acres of acquisition is projected under the program in these counties.

Other than the usual fish and game regulations, water-pollution controls, and local zoning regulation, the protection of estuaries is provided mainly through control over state-owned lands. The State Department of Conservation and Economic Development is responsible for estuarine land acquisition, and the State Department of Health for pollution control. Coordination

of state estuarine programs largely involves these
two agencies. Operating expenses for estuarine-
area protection for 1969 were $110,000; projected
1970 operating expenses are $130,000 (corresponding
figures for 1967 and 1968 were $93,000 and 142,000,
respectively.)

DEVICE FOR COORDINATED REGULATION AND ACQUISITION--THE AQUATIC-PRESERVE CONCEPT

Florida

Florida authorizes the designation of a "bulk
head line" along or offshore from tidal lands.[10]
Beyond such a bulkhead line, no filling or bulkheading
is allowed; in one county (Manatee), in addition,
no dredging is allowed beyond the bulkhead line.
Bulkhead lines are fixed by the local city or county
governing body, subject to the approval of the
Trustees of the Internal Improvement Trust Fund
(composed of the governor and six state cabinet
officers). A preliminary biological ecological and
hydrological study is required from the State Board
of Conservation. In this connection, the State
Board of Conservation has issued a circular containing
guides for evaluating marine productivity and adopting
standards for waterfront development. The Trustees
of the Internal Improvement Trust Fund placed a
moratorium on dredging and filling until these
studies could be completed.

A major recent development has been the establishment of a state-wide system of aquatic preserves
by the governor and the cabinet sitting as the Trustees of the Internal Improvement Trust Fund. (The
concept is described at length in Report Number 2
of the Florida Inter-Agency Advisory Committee on
Submerged Land Management, A Proposed System of
Aquatic Preserves.)[11] Eleven preserves were
established on the Atlantic Coast and fourteen on
the Gulf Coast. These preserves mean that no more
submerged land can be sold and no dredging and

filling permits to create waterfront real estate can be issued. Traditional uses--such as boating, swimming, sport and commercial fishing, bona fide navigation channels, and docks--would be allowed or continued.

The aquatic-preserve concept assumes that some of Florida's coastal areas are of special value to the state in their natural condition and should be dedicated in perpetuity as aquatic preserves, to be managed so as to protect and enhance their basic natural qualities for public enjoyment and utilization. An aquatic preserve will be characterized as being one or a combination of three interrelated types--biological (to preserve or promote certain forms of animal or plant life), aesthetic (to preserve certain scenic qualities or amenities), or scientific (to preserve certain features, qualities, or conditions for scientific or educational purposes). The preserves would be defined so as to include only lands or water bottoms owned by the state, although neighboring private lands might later be added pursuant to arrangements negotiated with the state.

The Inter-Agency Advisory Committee also reviewed all bulkhead lines in Florida and recommended that bulkhead either be relocated to, or set at the line of, mean high water, unless the public interest dictated otherwise, a recommendation that was adopted by the Trustees. Old and large conveyances of actual submerged land by the state to private individuals or firms and conveyances of actual submerged land as swamp and overflow land (because of erroneous meander line surveys) reportedly remain as major problems in estuarine management and conservation in Florida. As a remedy for these problems, statewide coastal planning and zoning have been considered but not yet carried beyond the discussion stage, and a priority system to identify activities needing waterfront locations has been proposed. In this context, the Chief of Survey and Management of the Florida Department of Natural Resources has indicated that golf courses, governmental centers, subdivisions, and expressways running the length of, or alongside, bays and sounds should be regarded as nonpriority uses.

EMPHASIS ON STATE AND LOCAL
COOPERATION IN COASTAL
WETLANDS PRESERVATION

New York

New York exercises regulatory controls in estuaries through a series of laws controlling fish, shellfish and wildlife, water pollution, and legislation that regulates dredging or other alterations of shorelines and underwater state lands. Further controls are exerted locally where underwater lands are owned by towns. The state lands under water are under the direct control of the Office of General Services. A permit from that office is required before any dredging of state lands can be carried out. The decision on whether or not this dredging is permitted is coordinated with the Conservation Department.

Under the Park and Recreation Land Acquisition Bond Act of 1960,[12] the State Conservation Department was authorized to purchase wetlands throughout the state and has acquired two tracts of nearly 250 acres of tidal marsh. Under the Fish and Game Law, the state may purchase land from any source,[13] and, under the Conservation Law, the Water Resources Commission may take land by eminent domain.[14]

The Long Island Wetlands Act permits the state government to enter cooperative agreements with the towns and counties on Long Island to preserve and enhance tidal marshes.[15] Where wetlands owned by towns or counties have been dedicated to conservation purposes, costs of maintenance and operations are shared by the state on a fifty-fifty basis with the local government. Cooperative agreements may also provide for development of dedicated wetlands by the State Conservation Department with its own personnel; 16,500 acres of wetlands are now under cooperative agreements with the townships. Program goals are to extend the agreements to about 16,000 acres of remaining township lands, which constitute the bulk of significant Long Island wetlands.

The State Conservation Department is primarily responsible for estuarine conservation programs. Condemnation powers are vested in the Water Resources Commission. Average annual state expenditures under the Long Island Wetlands Act are projected at about $15,000.

STATE THAT HAS MOVED MAINLY THROUGH REGIONAL PROGRAMS

California

California has recently concluded an extensive planning program for estuarine conservation in one area, the San Francisco Bay, begun with enactment of a legislative framework in 1965 and completed in 1969. The planning agency, the San Francisco Bay Conservation and Development Commission, was directed to study the Bay, prepare a comprehensive conservation and development plan for the Bay and its shoreline, and (as an interim measure) protect the Bay during the planning period by controlling dredging and filling by permits during the planning period.[16] Through 1966, the Commission issued twenty-five interim permits and denied five permits.

Presently, about 50 per cent of San Francisco Bay is owned by the state, 20 per cent is held by cities or countries, 5 per cent is federally owned, and 25 per cent is privately owned. This study commission completed twenty-three separate staff or consultant reports dealing with the Bay as a resource, with predicted future development, with planning for transportation and for land and water use, and with plan implementation. The annual Commission budget was substantial--for example, $243,924 in fiscal year 1967. A similar planning process has been proposed for the Humboldt Bay area in California, but it has not been activated.

The San Francisco Bay Commission, in April, 1968, published a comprehensive seven-volume report on <u>Powers and Money Needed to Carry Out the Bay Plan</u>.[17]

This report reviews, in detail, the alternatives available to the area for controlling Bay-filling activities and for planning, administering, and financing a program. The report provides an excellent source of information in depth for other states and areas. It includes a useful analysis of the pros and cons of the various revenue and organizational options and an extensive review of the legal precedents bearing upon regulation of estuarine land use.

In January, 1969, the Bay Commission published and submitted to the California State Legislature the San Francisco Bay Plan and the San Francisco Bay Plan Supplement.[18] Although the recommendations of the Bay Commission for a permanent regional government were not accepted in 1969, the Commission was itself made a permanent agency and authorized to continue its dredging and filling controls. (In addition to the work of the San Francisco Bay Commission, the state of California through its Resources Agency is now involved in preparing a comprehensive ocean area plan for legislative submission in 1972. The Department of Navigation and Ocean Development has been designated as California's Coastal Zone Authority.)

USE OF THE GOVERNOR'S POWER TO PLACE A MORATORIUM ON ACTIVITIES OF STATE AGENCIES PENDING COMPLETION OF ESTUARINE PLANS

Oregon

Oregon is currently in the process of developing a master Coastal Zone plan. It has so far completed its first comprehensive plan for an estuary, Yaquina Bay, and is working on Coos Bay.

Oregon found that, while this planning process was going on, some state construction agencies were proceeding along in routine fashion with highways and other improvements that would drastically change the natural environment of the coastline. In order to place a moratorium on such activities during the estuarine planning effort, the governor of Oregon issued an Executive Order directing the cessation of these activities as follows:

EXECUTIVE ORDER NO. 01-070-07

March 3, 1970

IT IS HEREBY ORDERED AND DIRECTED that all state agencies involved in construction or construction-related activities on the coast stop planning for or implementing any project that would modify the natural environment of the coast. This order covers sandspits, estuaries, and any coastal section where the project would exceed simple modification of an existing facility.

IT IS FURTHER ORDERED AND DIRECTED that all state agencies with regulatory responsibilities apply their authority in the most stringent possible fashion to insure complete protection of Oregon's coast.

IT IS FURTHER ORDERED AND DIRECTED that the Local Government Relations Division of the Executive Department and the Department of Transportation work with cities, counties and councils of government along the Oregan coast to initiate complete land use plans, specifically including transportation.

IT IS FURTHER ORDERED AND DIRECTED that the Highway Division and other appropriate state agencies provide staff and financial support to these local efforts.

IT IS FURTHER ORDERED AND DIRECTED that where local comprehensive plans are developed in a broad coordinated system that state agencies in carrying out their responsibilities comply with the priorities of these plans. Specific exemptions may only be granted by the Governor's office.

IN TESTIMONY WHEREOF, I have hereunto subscribed my name and caused to be affixed the great seal of the State of Oregon. Done at Salem, the capital, this 3rd Day of March, A. D., 1970.

(signed) Tom McCall
Governor

NOTES

1. Mass. Gen. L. Sec. 130-27A.

2. Mass. Gen. L. Sec. 130-105.

3. 349 Mass. 104, 206 N.E. 2d 666 (1965).

4. Maine Rev. Stat. Secs. 12-4,701 to 4,709.

5. Maine Rev. Stat. Secs. 38-541 to 557 (as added 1970) and Secs. 38-481 to 488 (as added 1970).

6. N.C. Gen. Stat. Sec. 113-226 (a).

7. N.C. Gen. Stat. Sec. 113-229.

8. N.C. Gen. Stat. Sec. 76-40.

9. N.J. Stat. Ann. 13:8A-1 to 18.

10. Fla. Stat. Secs. 253.122-123.

11. Florida Inter-Agency Advisory Committee on Submerged Land Management, _A Proposed System of Aquatic Preserves_ (Report No. 2 to the Trustees of the Internal Improvement Trust Fund), 1968.

12. N.Y. Conservation L. Secs. 1-0701 to 0715.

13. N.Y. Conservation L. Sec. 361.

14. N.Y. Conservation L. Sec. 423.

15. N.Y. Conservation L. Secs. 360 (e) and 394.

16. Calif. Ann. Code, Government, Title 7.2.

17. Legal aspects of the report on powers and money were covered in Volume I, "Regulation--Legal Questions," by Professor I. Michael Heyman. A summary pamphlet version of the full report is also available.

18. These plans are available from the Department of General Services, Documents and Publications, in Sacramento, California, for a combined price of $5.00.

ABOUT THE CONTRIBUTORS

David A. Adams is president of Coastal Zone Resources Corporation, Wilmington, North Carolina. He holds a Ph.D. in plant ecology from North Carolina State University and has served as Commissioner of the North Carolina Division of Commercial and Sport Fisheries and as senior staff member with the National Council on Marine Resources and Engineering Development.

Arthur W. Cooper is Professor of Botany and Forestry at North Carolina State University at Raleigh. He received the B.A. and M.A. degrees from Colgate University and a Ph.D. from the University of Michigan. His principal research interest is the plant ecology of the Coastal Zone.

Norbert Dee is a Research Associate with Battelle Memorial Institute, Columbus, Ohio. He holds a bachelor's degree in engineering from Marquette University and a Ph.D. in geography from the Johns Hopkins University.

Milton S. Heath, Jr., is Professor of Public Law and Government and Associate Director of the Institute of Government at the University of North Carolina at Chapel Hill. He received an A.B. from Harvard University and an L.L.B. from Columbia University and has served on the staff of the Governor of New York and the legal staff of the TVA

James C. Hite is Assistant Professor in the Department of Agricultural Economics and Rural

Sociology at Clemson University, Clemson, South Carolina. He holds an M.A. in history from Emory University and a Ph.D. in agricultural economics from Clemson and has done postdoctoral study with the Regional Science Group at Harvard University.

Maynard M. Hufschmidt holds a joint appointment as Professor of City and Regional Planning and Environmental Sciences and Engineering at the University of North Carolina at Chapel Hill. He received a B.S. in general engineering from the University of Illinois and a D.P.A. from Harvard University and was formerly Director of Research for the Harvard Water Program.

John Kissin is Assistant Professor of Regional Science at Harvard University. He received a diploma in economics from the University of Zurich and a Ph.D. in regional science from the University of Pennsylvania and serves as a consultant to planning agencies in the United States, Canada, and Great Britain.

Jack L. Knetsch is Professor of Economics and Director of the Natural Resources Policy Center at George Washington University, Washington, D.C. He holds a Ph.D. in economics from Harvard University and has served as agricultural economist with the TVA and as a research associate with Resources for the Future, Inc.

H. Gary Knight is Assistant Professor in the School of Law at Louisiana State University, where he teaches marine-resource law. He received an A.B. from Stanford University and an L.L.B. from Southern Methodist University.

Hugh W. Knox is Lecturer in Economics and Planning at the University of North Carolina at Chapel Hill. He holds a B.A. from Haverford College and is a Ph.D. candidate at the University of Pennsylvania. His principal research interest is the use of econometric models in regional planning.

Eugene A. Laurent is Assistant Professor in

the Environmental Resources Center at Georgia Institute of Technology. He holds an M.A. from the University of Nebraska, and a Ph.D. from Clemson University, Clemson, South Carolina. In 1969, he served as a member of the South Carolina Task Force on Tidelands Planning.

Frederick C. Marland is a Research Associate with the Marine Institute of the University of Georgia at Sapelo Island. He holds a Ph.D. from Virginia Polytechnic Institute and has served as a member of the faculties at West Georgia College and at the College of Charleston.

Francis H. Parker is Lecturer in Planning at the University of North Carolina at Chapel Hill. He received an A.B. degree from Wesleyan University and a Master of Regional Planning degree from the University of North Carolina.

E. Jack Schoop is Chief Planner, San Francisco Bay Conservation and Development Commission. He received a Master of City Planning degree from Massachusetts Institute of Technology and held planning posts in Massachusetts, Alaska, and California before accepting his present assignment.

James M. Stepp is Alumni Professor in the Department of Agricultural Economics and Rural Sociology at Clemson University, Clemson, South Carolina, where he is engaged in teaching and research in natural-resource policy and regional economic development. He received a Ph.D. from the University of Virginia and has served as a consultant to many national and regional planning and development agencies.

William A. Ward is a staff economist with the World Bank and a Ph.D. candidate in agricultural economics at Michigan State University. He holds an M.S. in agricultural economics from Clemson University, Clemson, South Carolina, and has been engaged in research concerning the regional income-distribution effects of natural-resource developments.